WELLS CATHEDRAL

AN ARCHITECTURAL & HISTORICAL GUIDE

ELSA VAN DER ZEE

Close Publications

Wells Cathedral
An Architectural & Historical Guide
by Elsa van der Zee

First published 2012
by Close Publications
Wells, Somerset, UK

Design by Iain MacLeod-Jones
www.imjdesign.co.uk

Printed and bound by Short Run Press, Exeter, Devon

Whilst every effort has been made to trace the owners of the copyright material reproduced herein, the publishers would like to apologise for any omissions and will be pleased to incorporate any missing acknowledgements in future editions.

A CIP catalogue record of this is available from the British Library

ISBN: 978-0-9572393-5-7

Cover image: South-East view of Wells Cathedral (Iain MacLeod-Jones)

To the memory of Peter Bird

Cathedral Architect 1994-2010

Contents

Illustrations

Additional photographs as follows:

Photographs by Michael Blandford on pp. 2, 7, 10, 13, 16, 29, 25, 31, 32, 36, 37, 38, 39, 41(l), 43 (top & bottom), 45(top), 46, 47, 51, 52, 53, 54, 58, 59, 60, 68, 71, 72, 74, 75, 77, 78, 85, 88 (top), 93,100, 101, 103, 104, 105, 111, 114, 116, 117, 125, 130, 131, 166, 178

Photographs by Andrew Featherstone on pp. 27, 28, 73

Photographs by Iain MacLeod-Jones on pp. viii (with grateful thanks to Lt Cdr Andrew Davies), 9, 17, 18, 29, 40, 42, 45 (bottom), 48, 50, 55, 57, 61, 63, 64, 70, 76, 79, 80, 81, 82, 86, 88 (bottom), 89, 90, 91, 92, 95, 96, 99, 102, 107, 108, 112, 113, 118, 119, 120, 121, 126, 128, 132, 133, 134, 135, 137, 138, 139, 140, 141, 142, 143, 145, 147, 149, 150, 152, 153, 154, 155, 157, 158, 159, 160, 161, 162, 163, 164, 167, 168, 169 (top), 170, 172, 173, 174, 175, 176, 177

Photographs by Owain Park on p. 80

Photographs by Peter Tudor on pp. 41 (r), 43 (middle), 44.

Photographs by Tim Williams on pp. 84, 110, 122, 123, 169 (2 bottom) 171

Acknowledgements

When Linzee Colchester wrote the *New Bell's Guide to Wells Cathedral* in 1987, it became for twenty-five years a major source of information for the cathedral guides and many others whose interest in the cathedral was more than a passing fancy. His knowledge, scholarship, enthusiasm and sheer love of the subject, provided inspiration for a whole generation. The idea for this present volume sprang directly from his work and it was only more recent archaeology, scholarship and interpretation which made some updating necessary.

Thanks are due to Anne Crawford (cathedral archivist) who acted with patience and understanding as editor/mentor and was ready to provide source material whenever asked. Thanks also to Canon Chancellor Andrew Featherstone, who read every word and was always helpful and encouraging, and to Frances Neale (former cathedral archivist) whose assistance and willingness to be consulted and provide valuable information at all times was a constant support.

The three major academic authors of recent times, Tim Ayers (glass), Warwick Rodwell (archaeology), and Jerry Sampson (early construction and west front) have all been most generous in allowing me full use of their writings. In addition, both Warwick Rodwell and Jerry Sampson have supplied me with photographs and illustrations to enhance the text. I am also most grateful to Jerry Sampson for the amount of time and enthusiasm he gave to walking round different areas of the building with me, allowing me to see through his eyes, a wealth of detail.

Photographs were also supplied by Michael Blandford, Iain MacLeod-Jones, Peter Tudor and Tim Williams, all of whom gave up time to create a comprehensive set of illustrations to complement the text.

Meg Corrick scrutinized every word in the book and made many helpful suggestions, particularly when my efforts at punctuation went astray, or a phrase needed clarification. Iain MacLeod-Jones spent much time with me on the design of the book and the improvement of the layout; way beyond the call of duty.

Last but not least I owe a great debt to Michael Haycraft (Clerk of the Works) who, through our many years of working together, gave me a much greater understanding of the building and its construction and above all, of the importance of sensitive conservation and craftsmanship

E. Z.

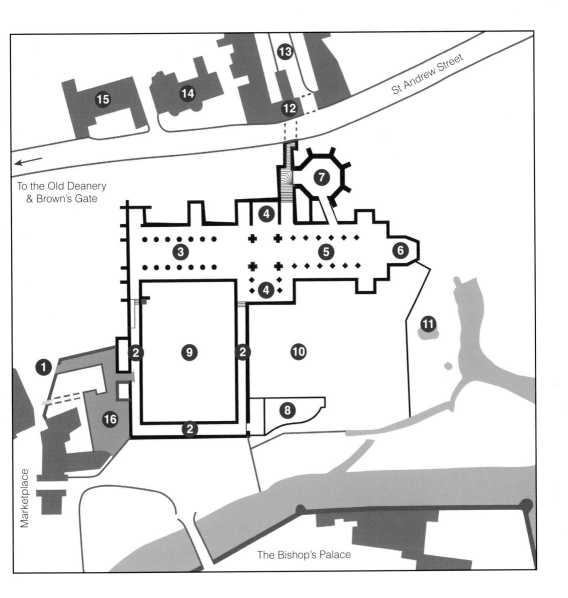

1 Entrance
2 Cloisters
3 Nave
4 Transepts
5 Quire
6 Lady Chapel
7 Chapter House
8 Friends Building
9 Palm Churchyard
10 Camery
11 St Andrew's Well
12 Vicars' Hall
13 Vicars' Close
14 Concert Hall
15 Museum
16 Shop and Restaurant

WELLS CATHEDRAL

AN ARCHITECTURAL & HISTORICAL GUIDE

ELSA VAN DER ZEE

Close Publications

The wells

Chapter 1
Brief Outline History

In the beginning...

It all began with water, essential to life and strong focus of religious faiths, in this case the springs or wells (which give the city its name) bubbling up from the limestone out of the silt, now to be found in the garden of the bishop's palace. The largest spring, isolated from the other three, is by tradition known as St Andrew's Well, and was possibly the focus, in pre-historic times of worship. Stone Age tools found in the vicinity point to interest in the site thousands of years ago, as people often followed water courses as an easier means of travel, and may indeed have worshipped nature spirits there. There is evidence too of Roman occupation but not a complete urban settlement. What *was* found, in the archaeological investigations of the late 1970s, was the base of a Romano-British mausoleum, with a stone-lined burial chamber still evident, most probably early Christian. The pure water of the springs gave a feeling of mystery and wonder to the site.

The first cathedral

It was not surprising therefore that King Ina of Wessex (688-726), in c.705, is said to have given permission for the founding of a minster church, with the ambition of christianizing Somerset. What is certain is that the bishop of the new diocese of Sherbourne, Aldhelm, founded this church. Sherbourne, a very large diocese, needed help if Christianity was to flourish throughout Somerset. Aldhelm remained closely connected to the area and died in Doulting in 709. Almost nothing is known about this early church: it may originally have been wooden. The first written evidence dates from 766 when Cynewulf of Wessex endowed 'the minster beside the great spring called Wielea (Wells)' with an extra eleven hides of land. The original building undoubtedly grew and was altered over the centuries and then in 909 given cathedral status when the diocese of Sherbourne was split. The first bishop, Athelm, was a Benedictine monk from Glastonbury, although there is no evidence that monastic rule ever pertained at Wells.

Most of what is known about this early cathedral is due to the excavations carried out by Warwick Rodwell in 1978-80. His work revealed that the early chapels, east of the main building, were aligned on the well of St Andrew and that a Saxon mortuary chapel was partially built over the Roman mausoleum. The alignment of all these early buildings was twelve degrees at variance

11th century drawing probably depicting the consecration of Wells Cathedral: the two barrels and heaving ground symbolize the springs

from the present cathedral, which is closer to true east-west. Only the eastern apse of the main building was exposed during the excavations but its direction pointed to a construction diagonally crossing the present cloisters with its front close to the market place. This was confirmed in recent archaeology when part of the atrium (forecourt) was found in the area of the modern restaurant and shop.

No further written evidence exists until after the Norman Conquest. The last bishop of the old cathedral, Giso of Lorraine (1040-88), was one of few prelates to survive in office, probably because he was a sympathizer of the new king, William of Normandy. Giso expanded the ancillary buildings so that the canons could live together in community. He also created another fair day in the market place on St Calixtus Day, 14th October, by co-incidence or not, the date of the battle of Hastings. His successor, John de Villula from Tours, removed his cathedra (seat) to Bath in 1090, perhaps because, also being a physician, he may have found more contemporaries to his liking there. In any case he had just been granted the abbey and all its possessions. It may also have been because of the resolution of the Council of London in 1075, naming the transference of several sees to cities, although at this period there was little difference between the sizes of Bath and Wells. Whatever the reason, John de Villula treated the canons of Wells with contempt, throwing a number of them out onto the streets as he destroyed the dormitory, refectory and cloisters of the old cathedral.

Robert of Lewes, Bishop of Bath (1136-66) was a vigorous builder and restorer. He rebuilt the abbey church at Bath and also worked to restore the old cathedral buildings at Wells, possibly adding nave aisles, with a view to enhancing its status again. He reorganized the Chapter at Wells and gave them a new constitution, now known as the 'Statuta Antiqua', which confirms that Wells then possessed dignitaries, canons, prebendaries, vicars choral, and choristers, who were sustained by a choristers' school and a grammar school for clerks. All this activity ceased on his death as there was a long interregnum. Henry II quarrelled with Thomas Becket who was subsequently murdered on 29th December 1170. Part of the king's ensuing penance was to fill all vacant sees at the earliest opportunity.

Order of Bishop Robert forbidding the erection of stalls in the
Nave or Porch of the cathedral during the three annual fairs

The present cathedral

Reginald de Bohun, then archdeacon of Salisbury, where his father Jocelin was bishop, was chosen as Bishop of Bath and finally consecrated in June 1174. Two archbishops, Peter of Tarentaise and Richard of Dover, the new Archbishop of Canterbury, officiated at St Jean de Maurienne in Savoy, as Richard and Reginald were travelling back to England from Rome. Bishop

Reginald was an international figure and had travelled widely for the Church. He had been a friend, first of Becket and then of Henry II. He was enthroned in his cathedral at Bath by Archbishop Richard on 24 November 1174.

His apparent decision to build a new great church at Wells in the, then entirely revolutionary, Gothic style, which he had seen in France, must have been in his mind from the very start. Work commenced in 1175 with the building at the east end of a Lady Chapel, so that services could be held while the church was being built. The work continued in stages progressing westwards, developing the Early English Gothic style as it continued. In 1191, Bishop Reginald was elected Archbishop of Canterbury but died within a month. By this time the building of his new prospective cathedral had reached the transepts.

Reginald was succeeded by Bishop Savaric (1192-1205), and the building continued after a short break, the second in the building sequence. These breaks occurred from time to time for various reasons, lack of money or available materials, and impetus from the bishop being in the forefront. Savaric spent much time on politics and his own aggrandisement. He acquired the abbacy of Glastonbury in effect by force in 1193, much to the resentment of the resident monks. He then felt entitled to call himself Bishop of Bath and Glastonbury but subsequently was absent from his diocese most of the time.

Savaric's lack of interest was more than compensated for by the zeal of his successor, Jocelin of Wells (1206-42) who was predominantly responsible

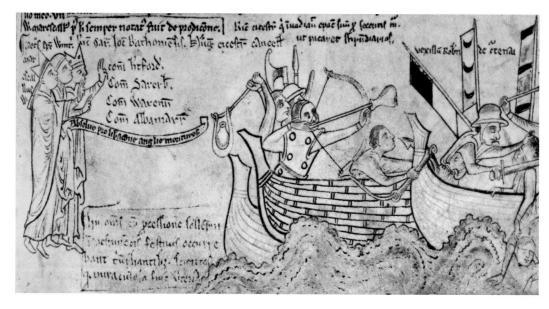

Bishop Jocelin blesses departing ships

for the building of the second half of the nave and the west front. Jocelin's family belonged to Wells. He himself was born in Launcherley, a little village just outside the city and his father later owned a house on the corner of the Liberty. His brother Hugh was Archdeacon of Wells and later became Bishop of Lincoln (not to be confused with the earlier St Hugh of Lincoln). Both Hugh and Jocelin were friends of King John and were his valued advisers, although he frequently went his own way. Consequently, his quarrel with the Pope over the choice of the new Archbishop of Canterbury affected both Hugh and Jocelin. The Pope's choice was Stephen Langton, who was then in Rome, but the king refused to let him set foot in England, causing the Pope to retaliate by placing the whole country under Interdict in 1208. By November 1209, despite trying to persuade the king to accede to the Pope's wishes, Hugh and Jocelin, together with four other bishops, went into voluntary exile.

Bishop Jocelin's crozier: brass inlaid with 13th century Limoges enamel

It is at this point that there was a considerably longer break in the building, which had reached just beyond the North Porch. This was in part the end of a planned phase of the building, but exacerbated by the absence of the bishop and lack of direction for a reduced work-force. Lack of funds inevitably also played its part.

In 1213, King John finally submitted to the Pope's request and Stephen Langton took up his seat in Canterbury; the exiled bishops returned. It is around this time that Adam Lock became master mason. By all accounts a gifted carver, his influence on the intricate carving of the foliage on the capitals of the western piers in the nave (beyond the North Porch) is evident. It is possible that building westwards did not start again until c.1220, when the new king, Henry III gave a gift of sixty oak trees for the cathedral. This may have galvanized all, from Jocelin downwards, into renewed vigorous action.

By 1219, Jocelin had surrendered his title to Glastonbury Abbey, which regained independence with its own abbot. Jocelin therefore was simply titled Bishop of Bath. He proceeded to apply to the Pope for cathedral status for Wells. Unfortunately as was often the case, the wheels of church diplomacy ground slowly, and Jocelin died in 1242, two years before the Pope finally authorized his successor Bishop Roger, to adopt the title of Bishop of Bath and Wells, as indeed is still the case today.

Not all dreams come to fruition; as with Jocelin, so Adam Lock was frustrated in the construction of the west front. His death in 1229, when probably only the plinth was complete, made it fall to his successor, Thomas Norreys, to carry forward and expand on his dream in a more elaborate, ornate style befitting a new era. By 1239, the west front was sufficiently high to be linked to the nave and be made weatherproof. This led to the dedication as a church, on 23rd October, even though there was unfinished work, such as the completion of the gable. Around this time, work on the chapter house complex was also under way: the passage to, and the outside walls of the undercroft, and the planning of the first part of the staircase which would ultimately lead to the first floor chapter house. Work on this seems to have come to a halt at Jocelin's death in 1242, and attention was concentrated on the west front. In 1286 under Bishop Robert Burnell, another builder bishop, the work resumed and the chapter house was finally completed in 1306. Bishop Burnell, following Jocelin's early construction of the adjacent palace, built a chapel on that site and an immense great hall, now a picturesque ruin (pictured opposite).

Intense activity ensued in the early fourteenth century and successive bishops concentrated on fund-raising, as for example, from the time of John Drokensford (1309-29) indulgences were offered to subscribers of the fabric fund. Also during Drokensford's episcopate, a division of power evolved so that from that era onwards, the dean had sole authority in the cathedral, while the bishop was pre-eminent in the diocese.

This was the beginning of the second great phase of building. Although the cathedral was deemed to be complete by the end of the thirteenth century, it also proved too small for some of the more ambitious liturgy, with grand processions being the order of the day. 1313 saw the beginning of the raising of the central tower with all its attendant difficulties of subsidence and dangerously cracking walls, leading ultimately to the creation of the 'scissor' arches (1338-48). At the same time work began on a Lady Chapel, east of the existing one, which was finished by 1326. As services could then be held there, it enabled work to begin on extending the quire and building the

retroquire as a link between the two new parts, thus providing a spectacular ambulatory for processions.

The Black Death

By this time another great building bishop had succeeded Drokensford; this was Ralph of Shrewsbury (1329-63). He was responsible for completing all the work on the quire extension by 1340 and building Vicars' Hall and Close, for his newly founded College of the Vicars Choral. The hall was ready by 1348 and the houses were certainly habitable by the time of his death. He also built the Choristers' or Organist's house, the gable of which can still be seen incorporated into the new building that houses the shop and restaurant. Having obtained a licence to crenellate he built a moat, gate-house and drawbridge with portcullis, and entire surrounding walls at his palace. All this occurred despite the Black Death raging in Somerset in 1348, when almost half the clergy died and therefore probably also a similar percentage of laity. Bishop Ralph temporarily took refuge in his manor of Wiveliscombe.

Final stages of building

William Wynford, a master mason of national importance was appointed in 1365. To a large extent he reconstructed the west end of the cathedral and its west gallery; completed the quire aisle vaults at the western end;

built the stone screens in both transepts; and at the west front, built the south-west tower as it is today. The latter was substantially funded by Bishop Harewell (1367-86) who also donated two bells, Great and Little Harewell. Wynford also changed the appearance of the Early English lancet windows in transepts and nave by introducing his design of perpendicular tracery.

Bishop Bubwith (1407-24), a man of some wealth, left money in his testament for the building of the north-west tower on the west front, in exact imitation of Wynford's design. He also enabled the building of a library over the top of the whole length of the remodelled east cloister, and the residue of funds was used for the building of the Almshouses still to be seen and occupied in Chamberlain Street.

The Bishop's Eye, one of Beckynton's gateways

Perhaps the greatest builder of them all both in Wells and on the national stage, was Bishop Thomas Bekynton (1443-65), a local Somerset man. Having first tutored the boy-king Henry VI, he became his trusted secretary and supervised the building of Eton College. He also had a hand in the building of Lincoln College, Oxford. In Wells, he concentrated mainly on the precincts and the building of a north wing in the palace, where the present bishop lives and works. Twelve houses were constructed on the north side of the market place, still known as the 'New Works', and three by Brown's Gate in Sadler Street. These were presented to the Dean and Chapter to enhance annual income for the maintenance of the cathedral fabric. He was also responsible for the four gateways: the Bishop's Eye, Penniless Porch, Brown's Gate, and lastly the Chain Gate. Perhaps his greatest gift to the town was a permanent supply of drinking water, piped by means of an underground conduit from the wells in the palace garden, underneath the cathedral cloisters and out into the market place. By the time of his death, work had also begun on a remodelled west cloister, fit to house the grammar school above it. This was not fully vaulted and completed until c.1480. His executors also used funds to heighten the chimneys of the houses of Vicars' Close.

There could not have been a greater contrast between Bekynton and his successor, Robert Stillington (1466-91). Of the twenty-five years of his episcopate he was absent for all but three and a half weeks. As a Yorkist supporter he was imprisoned on occasions during the vicissitudes of the Wars of the Roses; finally, because of his adherence to Richard III, he was imprisoned by Henry VII. When he did visit his cathedral, he gave orders for the building of a magnificent new Lady Chapel on the same axis as the present cathedral, thereby abolishing the old Lady Chapel-by-the-Cloister, a relic of Saxon times.

During his episcopate, work continued on the south cloister although it was not finished until 1508. Stillington's Lady Chapel, designed to be his memorial only lasted from 1488 until 1552, when Sir John Gate was granted the timber and lead from the roof, as well as of the great hall of the palace. In the case of the Lady Chapel, the condition seems to have been that the entire building should be removed to the last stone. The sale of lead and timber and indeed of brasses, was essential, since, after the abolition of the chantry chapels in the first year of Edward VI's reign, there were no longer sufficient funds to maintain the cathedral. Chantry chapels had previously brought in considerable income.

The English Reformation
No more significant building work was carried out until the Development Project of the beginning of the twenty-first century. However, gentle decay, neglect, restoration and repair continued over the next centuries in equal measure. The cessation of major building works coincided with the English Reformation. In the sixteenth century, Wells did not suffer unduly from the grasping hands of Thomas Cromwell, even though he was for a time titular dean. It was saved because it had never been subjected to monastic rule and had always been administered by secular canons. As a symbol of the new order of the Church of England, the first Anglican bishop, William Knight, chose as his tomb the pulpit in the nave, inscribed for the first time with an English text from the newly translated Bible (the Coverdale version). He died in 1547, the same year as the creator of the new order, Henry VIII.

The Tudor period was one of fluctuating fortunes in religious beliefs. The reign of the boy king Edward VI, which abolished the use of chantry chapels, was dominated in the first few years by his uncle Edward Seymour, Lord Protector and later Duke of Somerset. This gave rise to "protestant concepts more advanced than those of Luther". It was a period of religious austerity, a 'no frills' regime. Polychrome coloured stone, so vivid and dramatic in the Middle Ages was virtually obliterated both inside and out by white lime-washing (1550). In 1551 Dr William Turner was appointed dean. He was highly acceptable as a fervent protestant although not a fanatic; a physician with a deep interest in and wide knowledge of botany and herbal medicine. He wrote the *New Herbal*, the first work in English of its kind, published in 1568, which can be found in the cathedral library today.

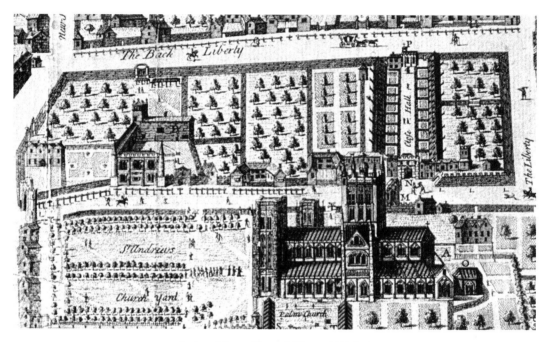

A detail from Simes' 'Plan of Wells':
the Deanery garden visible in top left corner

Dean Turner was wise enough to go into voluntary exile, together with Bishop Barlow, during the reign of Mary Tudor and the Catholic revival. He survived to regain his position at the deanery in 1561, where he remained until his death in 1568, a decade after Elizabeth I acceded to the throne and the unique English version of Protestantism was established. An approximation of Dean Turner's garden with its many herbs and medicinal plants has been recreated in the garden of what is now known as the Old Deanery. In 1591 Elizabeth affirmed and strengthened the authority of the Dean and Chapter, after a succession of largely absentee deans, 'to create, erect, found and establish the … cathedral church anew'.

Seventeenth century

It was in the seventeenth century that there was destruction, first from Cromwell's soldiers of the Civil War, and later in 1685, from those of Monmouth's rebellion. During the period of the Commonwealth, cathedrals were closed and bishops abolished. Dean Walter Raleigh (a nephew of the great adventurer and royal favourite) was captured in Bridgwater and later murdered by his gaoler at the Deanery and buried secretly at night under the dean's stall in Quire. A Presbyterian preacher called Cornelius Burges held sway in the cathedral and lived in the Deanery. Considerable looting took place including the stripping of lead from the roof.

At the restoration of Charles II in 1660, the building was in a sorry state. Dean Robert Creyghtone, who had been chaplain to Charles II in exile, was rewarded by this appointment on their return and for the last two years of his life, as soon as a vacancy arose, he was made bishop (1670-72). His was the task of making the cathedral functional and beautiful again. The organ was renewed and Dean Creyghtone personally donated the great brass lectern, complete with Bible, now to be found in the retroquire, and also the great west window in the nave, this last at a cost of £140. Just when all was progressing well, there came the set back of Monmouth's rebellion. Monmouth and his army were defeated at the Battle of Sedgmoor in 1685. The damage by the rebel

Portrait of Bishop Ken that hangs in the Long Gallery of the Bishop's Palace

soldiers to images in glass and stone statues was particularly noticeable in the Lady Chapel, the cult of Mary being anathema to the puritans. When they were finally surrounded and disarmed many were for a time imprisoned in the cloisters as well as in St Cuthbert's Church and the bishop's barn. The saintly Bishop Thomas Ken (1685-91) was frequently to be seen comforting the prisoners as they awaited their fate at the assizes of the infamous 'Bloody' Judge Jeffreys. He even accompanied Monmouth himself to the scaffold. Ken, a man of principle, refused to take the oath of allegiance to William of Orange and Mary (protestant daughter of James II) because he had already taken an oath to James II who had not legally abdicated but had gone into voluntary exile in France.

Eighteenth and nineteenth centuries

The eighteenth century was not noted for its religious zeal, and gentle decay and indifference might best describe the state of the cathedral. It did not help that some of the deans were almost permanently absent. However, the dawn of the nineteenth century saw a completely different spirit emerging, focussing on care and restoration of church buildings and a revival of interest in the Gothic style. In the 1830s, Benjamin Ferrey was architect at the cathedral (as also at the palace) under the enthusiastic leadership of Dean Goodenough (1831-45). It was he who was inspired to move the monuments from the main body of the church into the cloisters.

Ferrey was mainly responsible for the restoration of the nave and the Lady Chapel. Towards the end of Dean Goodenough's tenure, the so-called "Great Scrape" occurred; the systematic removal of the white lime-wash. Much of the original colour would have disappeared through contact with the lime but any that had escaped was almost obliterated by the vigour of the cleaning; some traces remain, mostly in crevices in the sculpted stone. The architect Anthony Salvin followed with a comprehensive reorganization of the quire, with a new organ, necessitating alteration of the medieval pulpitum, to support it. The first major restoration of the west front also took place (1870-74) under the direction, once again, of Benjamin Ferrey.

Education became a focus, especially in the Cathedral School for Dean Plumptre (1881-91), and his successor, Thomas Jex-Blake (1891-1911), who took a special interest in the library, to which he donated several books. He had previously been a respected headmaster of Rugby School. As dean, his wider interests included the supervision of the installation of new stained glass in the transepts and nave. Perhaps however, the most influential dean of the early twentieth century was Joseph Armitage Robinson (1911-33), who was transferred from the Deanery of Westminster to Wells. His maverick personality and wide scholarship, generated great energy and gave great impetus to the restoration of side chapels, the examining, repairing and restoring of historic glass both in the Lady Chapel and in the Jesse window in the quire, and in constantly

Cartoon of Dean Armitage Robinson

fund-raising through his well-connected, wealthy friends, to enhance the cathedral's beauty and draw Wells into the very heart of the Church.

...to the present day

In the same way, in the latter part of the twentieth century, the cathedral moved forward under the enthusiastic direction of Dean Patrick Mitchell (1973-89). It was he who drove the now famous restoration of the west front (1974-86) with its controversies over the relative methods of conservation or restoration and the best way of preserving the stone, badly eroded in parts. He combined the duties of Dean with those of Keeper of the Fabric which gave him comprehensive control over the west front project. Nobody can deny that it was a job well done and, although there are regular quinquennial inspections, no great catastrophes have been revealed and regular maintenance has coped.

The early twenty-first century, not to be out done, saw the most ambitious development of the cathedral site for centuries, first under Dean Richard Lewis (1989-2003), whose mantle was later donned by his successor Dean John Clarke in 2004. Both deans were strongly supported by the overall, practical grasp of the cathedral administrator, John Roberts (1995-2010). It was his energy which kept the momentum going even during the interregnum between the two deans.

The concept of a comprehensive modernisation of facilities had its origin in discussions c.1994/95. Permissions took seven long years to complete but gave the chance to refine both the idea and the detail and of course also to raise the necessary funds. The design architect was Martin Stancliffe, well known for his sensitive handling of ecclesiastical buildings old and new. Four sites were targeted: the masons' yard which had survived to date in ramshackle buildings with no proper workshops; a completely new building to house a song school and education centre (completely funded by the Friends of Wells Cathedral to the tune of £1.8m – an heroic effort by a small body of enthusiasts); the clearing out and opening up of the undercroft as an interpretation centre with a newly created passage for access; and finally an entirely new building for the shop and restaurant at the west end, thus enabling the cloisters to return to their original use, as a quiet, reflective space around Palm Churchyard, in which to walk, think, and talk.

Having taken about three and a half years to complete, all this was opened for the start of the visitor season of 2009 and dedicated in a moving service on 8 May that year. There is no doubt that it has greatly enhanced the experience of visitors and users alike.

The Friends Building: the Education Room

The Mary Mitchell Garden with cloister

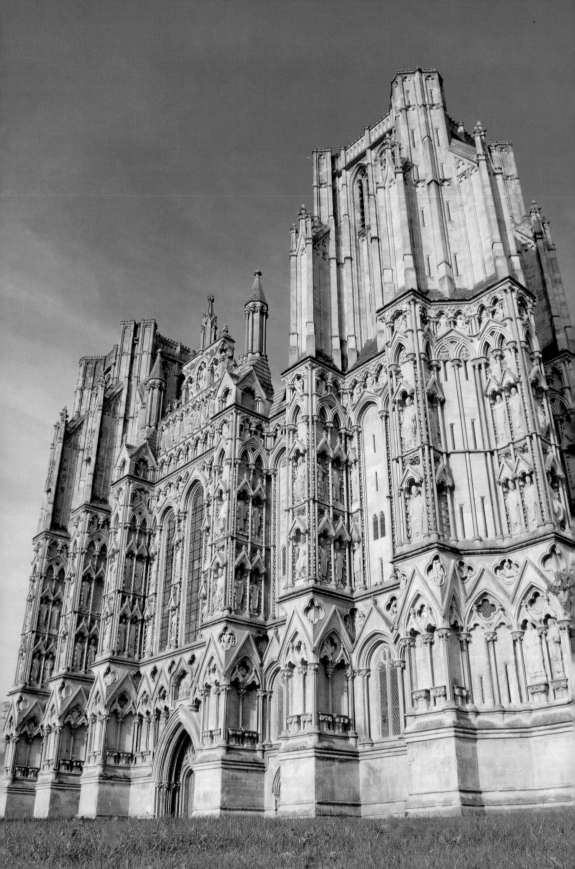

The West Front from Penniless Porch

Chapter 2
The West Front

From whichever side the cathedral is approached, whether from the east, under the Chain Bridge and along the north side, or from Sadler Street, through Brown's Gate at the far end of the Green, or from the market place by way of Penniless Porch, the west front draws the visitor in. Its great breadth sits squarely on the ground, dominating the Green in front of it; its solid square-topped towers further enhancing this impression. At the same time, the panoply of sculpture, reaching skywards from just above the plinth, right up to the top of the central gable, adds a feeling of lightness, joy and wonder to the structure. How much greater would the effect have been, when the medieval polychrome gave an increased three dimensional sense to the whole façade. The west front is perhaps the most all-embracing symbol of the cathedral itself, known and admired worldwide, with one the greatest remaining collections of medieval sculpture in the western world. Just under three hundred of the original four hundred sculptures remain.

Construction
In the nineteenth and early twentieth centuries there were several major restorations of the west front and a number of minor ones. When large scaffolding was erected, as in 1870-74, 1903, 1925-31, records were made and findings commented upon. It was not until the great restoration of 1974-86, however, that a really detailed scrutiny and recording of findings took place, greatly assisted by modern technology and detailed photography. Most of what is now known of the west front is supported by the, at present, definitive work: *Wells Cathedral West Front* by Jerry Sampson. He worked throughout the whole campaign in tandem with

the conservators, and gained a unique knowledge both of the structure (with access to every hidden space) and of the sculptures at the closest quarters.

There is no doubt that the west front was planned from the very beginning, at least in dimension if not in detail, and went up as a continuous process with the building of the west end of the nave. The nave arcade, the aisle vaults and the tower bases were all built up as a single unit and there is no sign of a pause in the building work up to the level of the aisle vaulting. At this point the great master mason Adam Lock was still in charge. He died in 1229, when certainly the plinth and probably the lowest tier of sculptures were in place. Many scholars have commented on the more elaborate change of style on the west front, often attributed to Lock's successor, Thomas Norreys, who had worked closely with him. It is also possible that the style evolved naturally as there is evidence of the same in the interior; for example, the increasingly elaborate undercut foliage on the capitals in the nave.

Certainly the footings were laid out in advance, including the first indication of the powerful buttresses, as had been the case throughout the building procedure, probably at the time of the completion of the north porch in c.1205/6. When the building campaign reached the west front, walls, niches and sculptures went up together, layer by layer, and generally the northern end was in advance of the south, as it had been in the earlier part of the building. Although most of the stone used, as elsewhere, is Doulting (inferior oolitic limestone) with contrasting shafts of blue lias (another local stone) at the lower levels, some white lias or beer stone has been used, as in two of the demi-angels in the quatrefoils. Also to be found mainly in the lower and middle tiers of sculpture is a considerable amount of Dundry stone from near Bristol. This might be because the sculpture workshop, set up because of the enormous increase of sculpted work on the west front (as opposed to the nave), could have come from Bristol where Adam

Replacement angel in beer stone

Lock was also known. Indeed, he is thought to have worked on the Elder Lady Chapel there. There is a letter of c.1218-20, in which Abbot David of St Augustine's, Bristol, asks the dean of Wells for the release of his servant "L", 'to hew out the seven pillars of wisdom's house, meaning of course our chapel of the blessed Virgin'. It seems to be generally accepted that the "L" referred to Lock and parallels have been drawn between the sculptural style of the Bristol Lady Chapel and the nave at Wells.

By the death of Bishop Jocelin (1242), the central section of the west front was more or less complete, although the gable above only existed in outline. The resurrection tier and its string course above were already progressing to the north and south. At this point there was a financial crisis, preventing a swift completion of the façade. This was caused by a major dispute with the monks of Bath Abbey, who had elected Jocelin's successor without reference to the canons of Wells. Litigation in Rome was inevitable and costly over many years. Indeed, not until 1263 was the burden of debt 'so nearly relieved' that Bishop William could assign once more monies from vacant benefices to the Chapter for use on the fabric. Even so, renewal of building work did not really get under way until 1286, when work on the chapter house was re-started. Jerry Sampson notes that in the intervening period between the death of Jocelin and the next big building push, the figure sculptors left Wells, having completed their work ahead of the building phase; they did not return to complete the gable figures or further statuary on the south-west tower.

In 1243, what is now the Green became the lay cemetery and an avenue of elm trees was planted, indicating that by then building work was not so dominant. Despite lack of funds however, some building work was still going on with a reduced workforce, probably on the gable. There is a description by Matthew Paris of the earthquake which occurred on 22 December 1248, when 'the stone "tholus" also, of great size and weight, which was being placed by the skill and care of the masons on top of the church of Wells for beauty's sake, was ripped from its place and fell not without damage to the fabric of the roof, and as it fell from on high it made a dreadful noise, striking great terror into those who heard it.' The strange word "tholus", originally meaning dome or cupola, probably in this case referred to the drums of the pinnacles, two of which survive, flanking the gable to the north and south. It is possible that such pinnacles were used to finish off the structure above the resurrection tier, as an extension of the great buttresses, the whole length of the front. This would reinforce the indication that originally, the west front was intended as a great sculpture screen, like an elaborate reredos or altar screen, without any idea of building the high towers to the north and south, above the resurrection tier. These were not added until the late fourteenth century in the case of the south tower, and early fifteenth century in the case of the north.

Jerry Sampson's idea of the early west front design

Design

Acceptance that the west front is like a gigantic dramatic screen is reinforced by the proportions, mentioned among others by Linzee Colchester; excluding the high towers and the gable, (in other words up to the string course above the resurrection tier) the façade is twice as broad as it is high: a perfectly proportioned rectangle. This was achieved by building the bases of the towers outside the nave aisles. It also made the west front exactly the same width as the transepts, which according to Jerry Sampson seems to have been an early design decision. The high towers themselves are quite unlike the highly ornamented thirteenth century front, although William Wynford, the designer of the south (Harewell) tower, did continue the line of the thirteenth century buttresses, up two thirds of the structure. He also replicated in essence the thirteenth century lancet windows. However, there is no ornamentation at all and the style is Perpendicular. In Bishop Bubwith's will it was stipulated that the north tower should be a direct copy of Wynford's design, although it does contain two west facing niches, one with a modern replacement statue of Bubwith himself. This tower seems to have used up stone which had been piled up in reserve and was not necessarily of the best quality. It has often been referred to as the rotten tower.

The Sculpture

This exceptional collection of thirteenth century sculpture, preserved where most contemporary work was destroyed or rebuilt in the fourteenth and fifteenth centuries, shows a great uniformity of style and therefore the existence of one sculpture workshop, drawing sculptors from near and far, each with their own traditions and predilections but nevertheless belonging to a group of carvers consciously striving for homogeneity. There are traces in the north porch of things to come even though this was the work of the existing Wells workshop; for example, the twelve deep niches (perhaps for the twelve apostles) were clearly made to house free-standing sculptures of considerable size.

Blocks of stone were often rough-trimmed only to fit a particular space, as would also be the practice today. This can be seen in the resurrection tier where not all fit the space comfortably and also in the quatrefoils, depicting scenes from the Old (north side) and New (south side) Testaments. This may be one reason why many have fallen out over centuries. Preliminary drawings were often made on large blocks and the shape of such a block might be in part preserved, as in the sculpture of the seated king (S187) with both arms thrust forward, where the arms preserve the position of the front face of the stone block.

The practice of coring out the backs of large statues was introduced to make lifting into position lighter and easier. The lifting gear to haul the statues into place must have been sophisticated; the statue was probably placed in some sort of cradle. Breakages occurred even in the early stages of shaping. These were repaired with dark red-brown mastic, so well bonded that it was still possible to carve the stone after the mastic had set. At least a third of the large sculptures, and certain smaller ones, were built with two or more blocks; mostly those made of Dundry stone. The blocks were joined with iron dowels, covered with molten lead to insulate against the corrosive effects of damp. Where the lead did not fully cover the dowel, problems arose as the expansion of the metal broke the stone. This subsequently also happened in the nineteenth and early twentieth century repair and restoration campaigns.

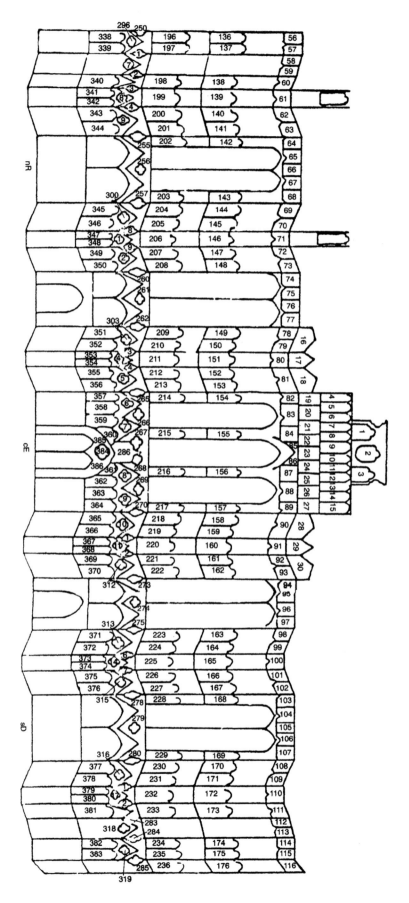

Plan of West Front statuary (Sampson)

24

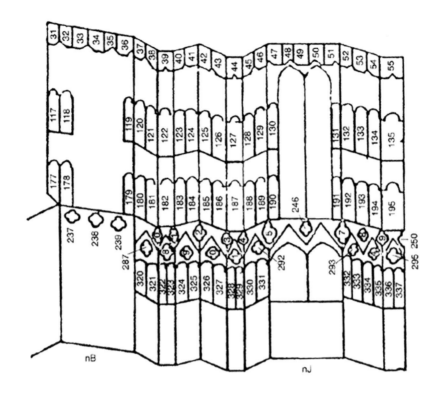

Plan of north-west tower statuary

West Front gable - the Apostles with St Andrew centre (S8-S12)

Painting

Enough traces of paint have been found to conclude that all the figures were painted and the backgrounds of the niches were coloured in a deep red. Initially all the stone was given a ground of ochre and then painted on top. The best preserved small areas of paint are those where the sculpted work was obscured by the niches and therefore protected. The best traces of decoration surviving are on figures S313, S257 and S132; all of these face north or east, away from the prevailing weather. It is also possible that large parts of the upper ashlar work were never painted at all, and although the figures of the resurrection tier contain traces of paint, there was none to be found in the gable. Perhaps this was again to do with funds running out after the death of Bishop Jocelin. Equally, no traces were found on the south tower which, as it was always slightly behind the north, was probably not finished when the sculptors and painters left. Much of the paint that has been found indicates pale or even white robes with decorative motifs on, for example, hems and stoles. This would help to give a strong three dimensional effect against the deep red background paint of the niches.

The greatest concentration of paint traces are immediately around the west door, that is, in the lowest tier of niches and the quatrefoils immediately surrounding the door. This, with the Madonna and Child in the centre, was the liturgical heart of the front and therefore probably given a much richer decoration, applied with the skill and care of the best painters. Reds, greens and golds abounded in foliage and figures, encompassing the central niche where Mary, the mother of God and also the symbol of the Church, is crowned by her Son.

A hypothetical reconstruction of the painted decoration of S132 based on surviving paint traces

Figures

Before examining the figures in detail, there is an unfinished inscription on the west face of the plinth, on the buttress to the left of the central door, at eye level. It reads:

> PVR: LALME: JOHAN
> DE: PUTTENIE: PRIEZ:
> ET: TREZE: IVRS: DE: ...

... and here it ends. The best guess according to Colchester, as to what the last line should have been is:

> PARDON: AVEREZ:

"Pray for the soul of John of Pitney and receive thirteen days indulgence." There was a John of Pitney, a chantry priest at Crewkerne, who died during the Black Death in 1348. Colchester suggests that the sculptor, failing to find a suitable tombstone, started an inscription on the buttress and himself died before finishing it.

A full catalogue of the statuary can be found in Jerry Sampson's *Wells Cathedral West Front*. The numbering he uses to identify them is adapted from that of Linzee Colchester. He prefixes statues with the letter S to differentiate between them and the empty niches. Only statues with clear attributes are named and many are identified as "a bishop", "a king" and so on.

The central section of the west front is clearly the main focus. Starting at the top of the gable, S2 is the figure of the seated Christ, flanked by two seraphim (S1 and S3), carved by David Wynne and placed there in 1985. Of the original, only the lower block remained and is now housed in Wells Museum.

Below is the row of apostles (pictured on p.25), with St Andrew in the centre, identified by his saltire cross and slightly larger than all the rest, perhaps to give him greater importance as the cathedral's patron saint. These figures are much later, dated to the third quarter of the fifteenth century. Between the apostles and the badly eroded nine orders of angels are a series of eight holes, probably for trumpets, to imitate the welcome of the heavenly host. Below the angels is the resurrection tier; people climbing out of their tombs and coffins (as pictured), some looking bewildered, some resigned, and

some joyful. This tier runs right round the front, including even the east face of the north tower. The two rows of larger figures represent the saints, the great and the good, waiting for the final judgement. Many of these are identifiable only as bishops, kings, knights, martyrs and even popes. However, on the lower tier, the two central figures in conversational pose, are known to be King Solomon (S216) on the right, and the Queen of Sheba (S215) on the left.

A string course divides all these figures from the quatrefoils. The upper row of quatrefoils contains stories from the bible. To the north of the great west door, they are from the New Testament according to St Matthew, who is represented by his symbol of a winged man. Many of these are missing and some badly worn. One, S257, 'Christ disputing with the doctors', has been replaced by a copy, carved by Derek Carr in beer stone. The remains of the original are in Wells Museum. On the south side of the west door are stories from the Old Testament, from the first part of the book of Genesis. More of these are still in place, with the birth first of Adam and then of Eve (S269 and S270) and the whole story of the Garden of Eden and the Fall being given prominence. Towards the south is a sequence of six quatrefoils depicting the life of Noah. Between the last two buttresses facing west is Noah at his work bench (S279) building the ark, and in the corner following is the ark afloat (S280) complete with a hierarchy of animals.

The lower quatrefoils are peopled by demi-angels. Most of these were in such poor condition that they were not put back at the end of the last restoration. Several of the originals are in Wells Museum and eleven have been replaced by modern copies carved by Derek Carr, using the same stone for each as the originals. The demi-angels are carved from several different types of stone, including the two in bright beer stone (pictured on p.20) which gives them undue prominence. The replacements were made possible by the generous donation of the Friends of the cathedral. On either side of the central door these quatrefoils are empty and it is possible to discern, in the background, another set of holes. These were for choir boys to sing the 'Gloria, Laus et Honor' during the Palm Sunday procession. With the demi-angels in front of the holes it would have seemed as though the very angels themselves were singing. A complete singing gallery is hidden inside the west wall, accessible at triforium level.

Above the central doorway is the niche containing the Coronation of the Virgin, but both figures are headless. Below, in the tympanum of the arch, is the depiction of the Madonna and Child, with new heads, sculpted by A. J. Ayers in 1970. This caused such a furore that the possibility of replacing the heads of the Coronation of the Virgin was abandoned. The Madonna and Child are flanked by two censing angels; these are among the earliest sculptures of the west front and hark back to the style of carving in the nave and in the north porch. The ten voussoir figures in the recess round the door arch are female and again created in beer stone. Each figure has a canopy above, quite plain except the upper two which contain angels coming out of stylized clouds, each holding a crown. On either side of the doorway above the lower string course are mainly empty niches which would have held the lowest tier of large figure sculptures. There are only two remaining at the far north end facing west (S339 and S340) and two at the far south end (S382 and S383). It is most probable that the damage was done by Monmouth's soldiers in 1685.

The best preserved figures of all are those on the north face, round the north tower. Among these are those known as the four Marys (S332-S335); Mary Cleopas, Mary Magdalene (carrying the alabaster box of ointment), Mary mother of James and Joses, and Mary the mother of Christ who is wearing a chasuble. Moving round, in the north-east corner are the five (originally six) figures which form the Gospel procession. These are deacons and sub-deacons arranged in pairs as thurifer and book-bearer alternately. In the two upper tiers of large sculptures are several with distinctive

The four Marys

attributes. On the far end of the east face in the upper tier is St Eustace (S118) wading through the waters of the Nile up to his knees, holding his two children in his arms. On the same level, on the north face of the buttress to the left of the north-west door, is a tall slightly elongated figure of a bishop. He is holding the top of his severed pate in his hands and could well be St Thomas Becket (S144). Between these last two figures, on the north face, are four magnificent knights in armour one of whom still has bright blue eyes which can be seen inside his visor (S123-126).

Meaning

Too much detail has been lost over centuries to ascertain exactly the intention of the builders in the most profound sense, and what Bishop Jocelin and Adam Lock discussed during the design phase will never be known. The most obvious interpretation is that the whole façade is a gigantic theatrical back drop for the Palm Sunday procession and also for the burial of the dead in the lay cemetery in front of the cathedral. Christ's entry into Jerusalem is re-enacted every year, with the waving of palms in procession, to the present day. The church represents Jerusalem, but by extension also the New Jerusalem, or heaven. So it is both in actual time and the hereafter. Looking at the top of the gable, it seems that the moment encapsulated in stone, is before the judgement of the last day, perhaps only minutes before. In the resurrection tier, the dead are still in the act of emerging from their coffins, even giving each other a helping hand, and there is no separation of the blessed and the damned, and no devil lurking. As that concept already existed in the thirteenth century, its omission could well have been intentional: more reassuring, more optimistic.

An analysis of the whole front including right round the towers, shows a wider interpretation than just its use on Palm Sunday. It also represents the history of the world, from the creation, as in the biblical quatrefoils to the south, through the first coming in the biblical quatrefoils to the north, right up to the second coming, shown by the resurrection tier and the whole gable with the seated Christ above. In the tympanum of the west door are the Madonna and Child, the central focus of the lower section: the Incarnation. Such as are left of the large figures of the lowest tier seem to have related to the early Church, of which the Madonna is a powerful symbol. Above the Madonna and Child, the Coronation of the Virgin points to heaven and the figures in the two middle tiers are saints and martyrs. In the centre above the Coronation of the Virgin are Solomon and the Queen of Sheba, inclining towards each other; they are central to the iconographic scheme. Solomon represents a type of Christ and the Queen of Sheba, a type of the Church. The gable itself, a third of the structure, represents the eternity of heaven, with the angels and apostles supporting the figure of Christ.

Looked at another way, there is a distinction between the sculptures to the north and those to the south. On the north side, these are temporal in the main; a long run of martyred kings for example, trampling their oppressors under their feet. On the south side, the spiritual representation is composed of clerics: priests, bishops and popes. The saints on the north side show some indication of the church universal according to Binski, as, not only are there English saints but also for example, St Eustace as already mentioned, and possibly St Olaf. Whatever their origin, the whole communion of saints are 'the living stones of the Church' (Binski) who, over the centuries have drawn in, in hope, those in search of comfort and peace. Coming upon the west front in the setting sun is an unforgettable experience, enhancing this feeling of mystery and serenity: an indefinable otherworldliness.

The empty nave in January

Chapter 3
Entrance and Nave

Visitor Entrance

Coming in through the modern entrance cloister near Penniless Porch, first opened in 2009, the serene tranquillity of the water garden is immediately apparent on the right. This area is known as the Mary Mitchell garden, since before the latest constructions, the garden as it then was, had been dedicated as a memorial to the wife of former dean Patrick Mitchell, who had died in December 1986. On the far side is the building which houses the shop and restaurant. This modern structure has sensitively incorporated the gable (all that was left) of the medieval Choristers' or Organist's house, which was originally built in 1354 and subsequently fell into ruin in the nineteenth century. It finally collapsed in the great storm of April 1870. Patrick Mitchell was consulted on the proposal to re-design the garden and there is a plaque on the south facing wall in memory of his late wife.

The porch to the old cloister where visitors now enter into the cathedral is the original point of entry for people in medieval times after the cloisters were built. Closed off for several centuries, it was unblocked during the modern development of this area. Turning to the left from this porch through a short arm of the west cloister, the west end of the nave can be seen through glass doors, which open automatically bidding all to enter.

The Nave (looking west to east)

Standing right at the back of the west end is the best way to see the intention of the design. It is the largest single space in the cathedral and being devoid of furniture, as it would have been (and still is in January every year), enhanced the feeling of magnificence and awe which influenced all who came in, all the more so with dramatic medieval paint everywhere. As Wells was the first cathedral in England to be built entirely in the Gothic style, the nave is essentially 'Early English Gothic' little altered from when it was first built. The proportions of width to height give a feeling of solidity of structure. The width from stone wall bench to stone wall bench is exactly 20.12 metres (66 feet or one cricket pitch length) or, as Colchester pointed out, in old measurement, one chain; and the height measured from the underside of the vault-rib at ridge level to the ground is identical.

There is however, a strong horizontal emphasis (not found in this way in mainland Europe), which draws the eye towards the east, the mysteries of the high altar and ultimately, in the mind, to the birthplace of Christ. This is achieved by the unbroken line of triforium arches with string courses above and below. Neither the so-called 'scissor' arch, nor the huge nineteenth century organ then existed to interrupt the continuity of the line and of course there was no raised sanctuary with an altar. Walking down the nave with its columns topped by stone carved foliage, as if through an avenue of stone trees, enhances this draw to the east. In the same way, the eye is directed upwards by a series of three levels of pointed arches or arrows, from arcade, to triforium, to clerestory: maybe to focus the mind also on God in his heaven. To those with few literacy skills, the visual impact dominated and led the way.

Construction
The entire building went up in phases, each time with a planned break in the building; the nave was built over two and a half such phases. As the construction went from east to west, the first two bays in the nave were part of phase three which also included the western side of the transepts; certainly this phase was finished by the very early twelve hundreds. Apart from the prevailing Doulting stone, here can also be seen a considerable amount of Chilcote stone. This is a much greyer, rougher stone, tougher than Doulting. The Chilcote quarry was owned by the cathedral and so enabled the building to continue even when Doulting stone was not available. The Doulting quarry was owned by Glastonbury Abbey and when the abbey was burned to the ground in 1184, all the stone from their quarry was required for the rebuilding of the abbey as speedily as possible.

The fourth phase, picking up from the low level buttressing at two bays into the nave, continued to just beyond the north porch (completed c.1205/6) reaching into the western part of the nave with buttressing to brace the completed parts. The construction always went up in horizontal layers. Here the break in building coincided with the Interdict (1208) and the exile of

Bishop Jocelin (1209) when most building stopped for a considerable time, although according to Jerry Sampson, the phase was completed even in the absence of the bishop, by a reduced workforce, in the early years of the Interdict. This period which lasted until 1220, is often referred to as '*The Break*' because of its length. In 1220, Henry III who had succeeded King John, gave a gift of 60 oak trees, initially to build a kiln, which seems to have kick-started the building with renewed vigour. The last, fifth, phase involved the construction of the western end of the nave together with the west front, already dealt with in the previous chapter. Despite all the breaks in the building however, there is a remarkable sense of continuity in the style, even though closer inspection reveals many small changes. This is particularly true in the carvings and after the mid-nave break, in the larger size of the stone blocks, when presumably over more than a decade, more efficient cutting and lifting gear had been developed.

Looking at the nave over all, it consists of ten equal bays, over a length of 46.09 metres (150 feet), divided by compound pillars or piers. Although these pillars are thick and sturdy, the old Romanesque drum-like shape has gone and the surface is broken up by a series of triple shafts, adding light and shade to the whole. Looking closely at the construction of these pillars, they consist of a square cross, with three shafts in each corner, and three shafts on each of the bars of the cross. Only the corner shafts are keeled, which gives a heightened vitality to the design. This pillar design is consistent throughout the building. The interior of each pillar is rubble filled, as also are the thick outer walls.

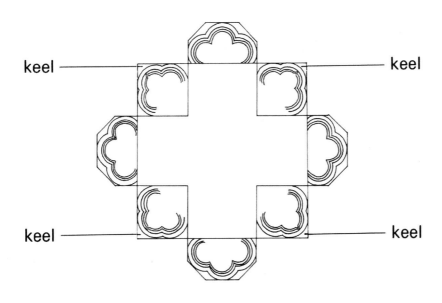

Cross-section of a compound pillar (from Colchester)

Looking up at the simple ribbed vault, again a feature of Early English Gothic, a blue and red leafy pattern can be seen throughout its length. This was rediscovered in the mid 1800s when much necessary cleaning and restoration took place. Two years were devoted to the so-called 'great scrape' (1842-44) to rid the building of its white lime-wash, originally applied at the time of the Reformation to cover all the dramatic medieval paint. A stencil of this pattern was made and the design reproduced throughout the nave and transepts. This decoration is based on the Persian Tree of Life, appealing to the Christian idea of eternity. When the plaster of the vaults was cleaned, repaired and repainted in the mid 1980s, more of this leafy design was discovered, revealing that not all the designs were identical, but evolved from east to west. However, for simplicity, it was decided to keep to the one design reproduced by the restorers of the nineteenth century.

The one scissor arch which dominates the nave so effectively will be dealt with in the next chapter, as it is essentially part of the crossing. However, the Rood figures belong to the nave area. Originally, similar figures were placed there in the latter part of the fifteenth century by Dr Hugh Sugar, treasurer of the cathedral. These may indeed have replaced even earlier figures (Colchester). During the Reformation, these figures were destroyed, with only the stump of the wooden cross remaining in its stone socket. As an experiment, Dean Armitage Robinson placed a simple wooden cross there in 1912, which was replaced c.1920 with the present, slightly more elaborate cross and the Rood figures of the crucified Christ, flanked by Mary his mother on the left and the beloved disciple John on the right. These were designed by the consultant architect, Sir Charles Nicholson and carved by Guglielmo Tosi of Brompton.

Above: the Rood figures
Opposite: the vault pattern with singing gallery visible in the centre right

Coming down to the mid-way point of the nave and looking high up on the south side, at clerestory level, a 'singing' gallery can be seen in the fifth bay from the crossing, belonging stylistically to c.1450. This has at times been described as a minstrels' gallery but there is very little room for instruments or people. More likely is its use for an angel choir of boy trebles, no more than two or three in number. Its use could have been for certain dramatic performances, as for example, a nativity play. What more dramatic effect could there be than the angels from on high singing, "Glory to God in the highest, and on earth, peace." It is worth noting also, that this gallery is directly opposite the north porch, the entrance of the great canons or dignitaries (the *quinque personae*, or the members of the administrative chapter) into their cathedral. It is not inconceivable that on special occasions a few choirboys might climb the spiral staircase and, at some risk to their safety, make their way to the gallery, where angelic singing might welcome the chapter canons in. Nowadays, with so many health and safety regulations, this gallery is no longer in use. It is not easy to be "angelic" while wearing a safety harness and a hard hat!

Corbel of a bishop

Also on the south side, in the seventh bay from the crossing are two distinctive corbels in the spandrels of the arcade; one of a bishop and the other of a king, representing the twin powers of church and state. Carved in the early fourteenth century, these corbels, which are flat on top, were undoubtedly the base supports of a wooden platform, which carried an early, small organ. Such an early instrument would have been used to keep the notes of the plainsong chants in tune, or to denote a change of key during processions. At triforium level, some of the door furniture in the arch between the two corbels still exists: a rather precarious entrance for the organist to gain access to the platform. No wonder this arrangement only lasted for about fifty years, when, with the building of the stone pulpitum (c.1335), the organ was transferred to its present day position; of course, nowhere near the size of the great Victorian instrument in evidence today.

The Break

Just to the west of the level of the north porch, is considerable evidence of a longer break in the building than was usual at the end of a planned phase. Many people have enjoyed playing detective and noting all the changes in this area, even very small ones. Already referred to is the change in size of the stone block, more readily visible on the south side. The original size could be carried by one man if necessary, but certainly not the larger ones. This change did not occur abruptly, as the smaller blocks, ready cut and stored, were still being used up. These smaller blocks have diagonal tool marks, whereas in the case of the larger block, a toothed drag or comb has been used to give a vertical finish to the stone.

Turning to the north side and looking up to the carved roundels in the spandrels of the triforium arches, those towards the east are all countersunk within their roundels. To the west, these roundel carvings are flush with the ashlar (stone block) of the wall. In the same way, there are three different designs of carvings in the nave triforium tympana: roundels at the extreme eastern end, followed by triangular curling patterns inhabited by creatures, followed at the western end by symmetrical foliage about a centre line. Just below, are the hood-moulds of the main arcade. East of the mid-nave break, these are finished off with small carved heads, whereas to the west, there are no head stops and the hood-moulds meet at points in mitre-joints.

The three types of tympana design

The capitals at the top of the nave pillars also change as they progress westwards. At the eastern end, fairly simple carved stiff-leafed foliage can be seen, very much 'inhabited' by all sorts of creatures and people. To the west there is much less 'habitation' but the foliage becomes very elaborate, with great swirling curls and deeply undercut. Even in the roof, not visible from the ground, there are changes in the jointing of the timbers, progressing from an ordinary notched lap-joint (to prevent slippage), to a secret (hidden) notched lap-joint.

The Western End

This area is the most altered from the Early English Gothic, as it was the pre-occupation of master-mason William Wynford in the late fourteenth century at the same time as he was designing and building the south tower on the west front. The mullions of the great west window were renewed, as was the parapet or balustrade of the open west gallery, situated immediately under the window. On either side of this window, there were originally freestanding blue lias shafts with decorative fleurons behind (as on the west front). These shafts were resting on the still intact lias abacci. Facing the window, signs of the remains of hacked off fleurons can still be seen, high up on the right, behind Wynford's shaft. Wynford replaced the blue lias shafts with close-fitting Doulting stone, almost as an extension of the round shafts which issue from the sloping west wall. Inside this sloping wall, is the singing gallery, already mentioned in the previous chapter. This adaptation was all about creating a more 'perpendicular' look, so apparent in Wynford's work. He also filled the original, plain lancet windows with perpendicular tracery throughout the length of the nave and beyond.

The singing gallery

Still facing west, the use of different stone can be seen in four thick shafts, two on either side of the columns which flank the great west door, fashioned in Draycott conglomerate. At the lower end where people's hands have felt the stone, the surface has become highly polished and looks like marble.

Further up, the surface is dull and dusty looking. Other examples of Draycott conglomerate can be found in five monumental floor slabs within the cathedral, all dated between 1644 and 1655. It is not known whether the shafts themselves are part of the original construction or maybe date from the middle of the seventeenth century. On the far right of the west end is a pair of eighteenth century doors which shut off the base of the north-west tower. This area has been in the past a chapel, the bishop's consistory court, the choristers' vestry, and the shop. Now it is used to store equipment. Hanging above the doors, is a late thirteenth century wooden pyx-canopy, designed to hold the pyx with its consecrated sacrament. Delicately carved in oak, there is still evidence of medieval red and white paint remaining.

The Glass

Very little medieval glass remains and probably there was not any until the late fourteenth century adaptations. Before then the lower windows may have been covered by oiled cloth, to keep out at least some draught, and the upper windows covered by wooden shutters. One or two examples of medieval glass remain in the top traceries of the clerestory windows. Particularly noteworthy are wonderfully feathered six-winged seraphim, both at the eastern and the western end of the south side.

Two of the feathery seraphim

Not just their wings but their bodies are covered in feathers, and their beautifully detailed bare feet are balancing on wheels.

The great west window, originally given by Bishop Harewell, was replaced by Robert Creyghtone, first dean (1660-1670) then bishop (1670-72), after the restoration of Charles II. The two outer lights are distinctly of this period. The centre light was redesigned by A. K. Nicholson in 1931, although very much in keeping with the original design. The window depicts the Transfiguration of Christ, with Moses and Elijah at the top on either side of the Christ-figure. Beneath, on the south side, is a seventeenth century representation of King Ina of Wessex, the founder of the original minster church; and in the north light, Bishop Ralph of Shrewsbury, the builder of Vicars' Close. Nicholson continued this scheme by producing a likeness of Bishop Robert Creyghtone

Great west window left light, with King Ina (middle figure)

in the centre light. This window has always suffered from the prevailing westerly wind. In particular, the centre light was destroyed in the great storm of 1703, when the Eddystone lighthouse collapsed and, in Wells, Bishop Kidder and his wife were killed by the fall of a chimney through the roof, as they lay asleep in the palace. The amount of ferramenta (metal bars) clearly visible, shows how much the window has to be protected from the west wind, blowing up from the Bristol Channel.

Still at the west end to the south and to the north, above the smaller doors, are nineteenth century windows by James Powell and Co. On the south side they depict the Annunciation and the Visitation of Mary to her cousin Elizabeth. On the north side are Christ's Baptism and the Presentation of Christ in the Temple.

Further towards the east, in the south nave aisle, are four two-light windows by Kempe, inserted in 1905-06. Kempe is always recognizable by his emblem of a wheat-sheaf, positioned somewhere in the glass. Reading from west to east, the first window contains St Matthew and St Mark, with below, the shepherds at the manger. The second window has St James the Less and St Philip, with the Adoration of the Magi below. The third window depicts St Peter and St John, with The Women at the Sepulchre beneath. In the tracery lights of this window are fifteenth century glass images of two knights in armour. The window nearest to the east has St Stephen and St Paul with, underneath, Christ's command to Peter.

The Capitals

Already mentioned in general outline, but worth a more detailed look, are the carved capitals of the pillars. They show a wealth of imagination and inventiveness, not on religious themes, but they simply manifest creative joy. It would appear that the masons carved whatever took their fancy.

Starting from the west end on the north side, the second free standing pillar has a female head appearing out of a flute-like shape, a double bodied lion with one head munching the leaves and two dragons with leafy tails. The third pillar on the north has a pair of birds and dragon heads with bird-like bodies and leafy tails. Still on the north, the fourth pillar has a goat's head with long downward-curving horns, a ram's head with short curly horns (difficult to see) and

two birds pecking the foliage with a grotesque head between them, and also two birds preening their feathers. These are all quite small. The fifth pillar has two beasts snarling at each other and two bird-like dragons, one wearing a coronet, again with leafy tails.

Crossing to the south side, the fifth free-standing pillar from the west has two dragons fighting, one clearly thrusting a spear down the other's throat; he has a nasty expression on his face and the wounded dragon backs away with wings outspread. In addition, there are two small devil heads with long necks and one large one; all of these have asses' ears. The seventh pillar on the south side depicts two birds with long twisted necks and human-like heads, one wearing a jester's cap. The eighth pillar on the south which now joins the pulpit and the chantry chapel has a lion, now headless, attacking a man, a lyre bird, and an eagle which has also lost its head.

Crossing once again to the north side, the sixth pillar from the west has carvings on almost every shaft with big, bold images. It contains a lion roaring over its back; if you look closely inside its open mouth, its tongue is pink, a leftover of original medieval paint. Walking around this pillar anti-clockwise there are two monkey-faced dragons, a wonderful ram with curly fleece and horns, a man with a bird's

body, a demon-type form, a bovine creature and a peasant, two pigeons preening their feathers, and two back-to-back dragons. This splendid array of sculpture would be the first to be seen when the canons entered the cathedral from their porch.

On the eighth pillar by the chantry chapel, is a small carving of a farmer, cudgel in hand, stalking a fox which has run away with the farmer's goose in its mouth. On this same pillar, inside the chantry chapel are a spoonbill with a frog in its beak, and a devil-like creature holding a large fish in one hand and a billhook in the other. On the final pillar at the east end of the chantry is a wonderful stout packman carrying his wares, including a large string of beads and beyond him, a corpse-like figure leering down malevolently, with his hands on his knees. Some of the capitals of the north quire aisle are also worth a look; a peddler-type figure near the virgers' vestry, and one known as 'the market scene' (below), two sets of triple shafts west of the north porch, which on close inspection has some very curious features!

The Chantry Chapels

The two chantry chapels at the east end of the nave appear similar although they are more than half a century apart. Both are hexagonal and both are perpendicular in style. On the north side is the chantry dedicated to the Holy Cross. Here Bishop Nicholas Bubwith (1407-24) is buried, having made his bequest and thereby the chapel being finished, before his death. On the west wall inside the chapel is the earliest known representation of the arms of the See, in this case impaling the arms of Bubwith. The figure of Our Lady of Walsingham, on the central pedestal above the altar, was placed there in 1985 after a diocesan pilgrimage to the Walsingham shrine.

On the south side, the chantry was built with a bequest from Dr Hugh Sugar (d.1489), treasurer of the cathedral and later Vicar General to

Bishop Stillington. It is dedicated to St Edmund of Abingdon, Archbishop of Canterbury (1233-40). Inside the chapel at the west end are two further capital carvings. On the right is a curious owl, head tilted, and on the left a man carrying a scroll. The architectural style represents the very end of the perpendicular period, with the fan-vaulting of the canopy and intricately carved stone above the niches. It also contains four rebuses (three small and one large) of Dr Sugar's name. The angel's shield carries a medieval doctor's hat surrounded by three sugar cones (right).

Chantry chapels, created to say mass for the dead, to ease the soul through purgatory, were a great focus of the later middle ages, when the idea of purgatory was almost obsessional. They were abolished within the Church of England in the first year of Edward VI's reign (1547) as part of a stricter Protestant ethic. Only the wealthy could afford a splendid chapel and monies to pay for a chantry priest. This did not equate with Christ, the advocate of the poor and needy; besides there was no reference to chantries or purgatory in the Bible.

Bishop Knight's pulpit tomb

Following the abolition of chantries, the Sugar chantry was used to create an entrance for the new pulpit, built out from the north-west corner. It is also the tomb of Bishop William Knight who died in 1547, the same year as the creator of the Church of England, Henry VIII. Bishop Knight chose the pulpit for his tomb as a symbol of the new order. A new Renaissance style (in contrast with the heavily sculpted chantry chapel behind) with straight classical lines emphasizes this new order. The pulpit also carries the first carved English text, from the Coverdale 'Great Bible' of 1539. It is part of Paul's second letter to Timothy. As the carver ran out of space, certain abbreviations were introduced and Timothy, obstructed by the pillar became Timo. One minor change to the in 1611, still visible, was the altering of the word IMPROVE to REPROVE in accordance with the translation of the new King James Bible. Also of note is some bold graffiti with the date 1654, the period of the Commonwealth, when use of the cathedral was suspended and much desecration took place.

Left: textual change of 1611. Right: mutilated coat of arms of William Knight

On the pavement west of the pulpit are two blue lias ledger stones with the medieval brasses ripped out. One or two brass tacks can still be seen in place. After the abolition of the chantries, those monies went to the crown, depriving the Dean and Chapter of funds for the repair of the fabric. On this occasion the brasses were sold to renew the lead on the nave roof. There are no medieval brasses left in the cathedral; all those remaining date from the seventeenth century and later.

Two other ledger stones of the early thirteenth century have incised floriated crosses; one on the north side below the sanctuary, and one on the south side in the fifth bay from the east between the two pillars. The latter contains indents at the crossing of the bars, where costly jewels would have been: one large oval shape in the centre, surrounded by eight small round ones.

In the centre of the nave, at the east end is a more modern, commemorative stone, to Ina King of Wessex, credited with the founding of the first minster church in c.705. This was put there at the instigation of Dean Armitage Robinson in 1916, to remember the founder of Christian worship in Wells. The ledger stone immediately by the door to the north porch, in the north nave aisle, is one that always attracts interest. It bears the name of Thomas Linley and his daughter Elizabeth Ann Sheridan, wife of the playwright Richard

Brinsley Sheridan; also of Elizabeth's sister, Mary Tickell and of Elizabeth's illegitimate infant daughter, nobly adopted by Sheridan. Before her marriage to Sheridan, Elizabeth had been an accomplished singer, performing among others, for George III. Among her many well-connected friends was Georgiana, Duchess of Devonshire.

From the historical artefacts and phases of Gothic architecture, the sanctuary with its altar shows the influence of the modern age; of a working and still evolving church. The raised sanctuary was dedicated in 1970. The use of a nave altar dates from the Second World War. The furniture for choir and priests is modern (1997), made by Illingworth and Partridge of Dorset, in limed oak, to reflect the honey-coloured Doulting stone. In the year 2000, to celebrate the Millennium, altar frontals for the nave and quire, together with vestments for the Eucharist were commissioned. Every season of the church calendar, with its own colour, is represented. The nave frontals were designed by Maurice Strike and the high altar frontals by Jane Lemon. The work was carried out by the Royal School of Needlework and the Sarum group of embroiderers. All were paid for by public subscription.

The Pentecost altar frontal

The transepts and crossing from the south

Chapter 4
Transepts and Crossing

Construction

The building of the transepts and crossing overlaps phases two and three of the early construction and was completed by c.1200. The eastern aisles are part of the quire build (phase two), with enough buttressing in the transepts themselves to give support to the finished works. Phase three was the building of the main part of the transepts and central tower up to the roof-line, continuing, with buttressing, into the first two bays of the nave.

It is unusual for transepts to have aisles both to the east and west; the model for this probably came from St Paul's in London. In both transepts, the eastern aisles were occupied by two chapels; on the north side, the first dedicated to The Holy Cross and the second to Corpus Christi; these no longer exist. In the south transept are the chapels of St Calixtus and St Martin, still intact. In both eastern aisles, there are doors near the western side. In the case of the south transept, this is blocked but on the north side the door is now the entrance to the chapter house steps. During the construction period, however, the eastern aisles with their doorways might well have been used as a processional way, for entry into the quire. It is also quite possible that some kind of vestry or even sacristy (Rodwell)was intended, as the doors faced outwards into spaces beyond. On the north side, evidence of roof-mouldings can still be seen on the other side, above the door. There were windows above, blocked in the early thirteenth century on the north side and later tracery added on the south.

As mentioned before, the use of Chilcote stone, because of the great fire at Glastonbury Abbey in 1184, is evident for the first time in the transepts;

the pillar dividing the chapels of St Calixtus and St Martin in the south transept shows the earliest use of this stone. Fortunately, as Chilcote stone is very difficult to carve, enough Doulting stone had been stockpiled to allow for use in the capital carvings, resplendent in both transepts. Although Chilcote stone is evident throughout and even in the eastern part of the nave, as soon as the Doulting quarry became available once more the use of Doulting stone as the standard material of construction was re-introduced. What is most remarkable is the continuity of style throughout the building and it is known by the masons' marks that a few masons from the transept phase were still working in the western part of the nave.

South Transept
Both chapels in the eastern aisles now form part of a County War Memorial, originally for the men of Somerset who gave their lives in the First World War, later incorporating those of the Second World War, as the inscription in gold lettering, linking the two chapels, bears witness.

St Calixtus

Virgin with lilies

This chapel is made available for private prayer and offers a quiet retreat from the bustle of the south transept. Above the altar is a crucifixion group carved by Guglielmo Tosi as a study for the Rood carved by him on the scissor arch at the east end of the nave. On the south side of this chapel is a fine alabaster tomb of, according to Colchester, an unidentified cleric. At present it is referred to as the Boleyn tomb; Thomas Boleyn was precentor of Wells (1451-1472). Whether it is him or not, the tomb is splendid enough to have been created for a priest of some importance. The front of this tomb has some fine alabaster carvings. At the eastern end is a representation of the Annunciation; a delicate Virgin with lilies in the foreground. In the centre are three canons, mourning. At the west end is a representation of the Holy Trinity, popular at the time. God the Father cradles his crucified Son and there are three holes in the top right-hand corner, where a dove, the Holy Spirit, might have been fixed. The carvings of this tomb had suffered over the centuries, and in the restoration of the 1840s all the heads, with the

The Holy Trinity

exception of the Annunciation panel, were replaced, as well as some minor details in the Holy Trinity panel. Some further conservation is being considered. The glass was designed by A. K. Nicholson in 1922 and shows, in the main lights, St Calixtus and King Arthur. In the narrow left-hand light are the arms of the See, the badge of the Somerset Light Infantry, and the arms of the City of Wells. There is some fifteenth century glass in the traceries.

St Martin

Here the Rolls of Honour of those who died in both World Wars are kept. The pages can be turned for those seeking a relative, by request to a virger. The altar reredos, designed by cathedral architect Sir Charles Nicholson (1909-1949), was again carved by Guglielmo Tosi as part of the memorial of the First World War; it was painted as part of the commemoration of the Second World War. On the south side is the tomb of William Bekonyll, a prebendary of the cathedral (1432-48). To the west of this, part of the badly blocked doorway can be seen. In front of the altar, in the floor, is a rare example of a lead, vertically-incised memorial slab to John Grene, who was a canon of Wells (1372-1410). The glass in the south window shows St Dunstan with St Edward the Confessor in the two main lights. The east window depicts St George with his cross, and above in the tracery, the slaying of the dragon. The middle light shows St Martin of Tours with, in the tracery above, St Martin dividing his cloak with a beggar. The right-hand light is of King Alfred, with the badge of the Royal Navy below, and in the tracery above, the first English fleet being built. These windows were also designed by A. K. Nicholson, brother of Sir Charles.

The de Marchia Tomb

On the south side are two structures associated with Bishop William de Marchia or William of March (1293-1302): his tomb and a reredos or altar canopy, possibly part of a shrine which should have been placed behind the high altar in the quire. Both of these contain a substantial amount of medieval colour; there are even traces of heads and basic red paint immediately west of his tomb, under the crenellations: no doubt some form of wall painting. Altogether this wall must have been a splendid spectacle. William de Marchia was for a time a candidate for canonization, but the petition ultimately proved unsuccessful and all attempts were given up after the death of Bishop John Drokensford

in 1329. It is possible that the canopy east of the tomb was placed there after this attempt, to give some kind of focus to prayer. Wells could have done with a saint, as pilgrims brought in much needed revenue and relics at Wells were few. Interestingly, behind the back wall of the canopy is a relic chamber, accessed from the passage above. The relics could undoubtedly be glimpsed through the slits in the reredos; a black background can still be seen. His tomb, for the early fourteenth century, is lavishly decorated with statues, now headless: an edifice suitable for a prospective saint! In the south wall of the canopy structure, where an altar might have been, is a brass plaque commemorating Jean Viscountess Lisle (d. 1463). She is in fact buried in the crossing in front of the pulpitum and does not belong to this reredos at all.

Continuing to move clockwise, within the crenellated wall is a door leading up to a small chamber which was probably used as a strong-room, or even the escheator's office. There is a corresponding door and room in the north transept. Both rooms had iron-clad doors for greater security. To the west of the door on the south side is another door which leads up to the medieval library above the east cloister. This will be described in a subsequent chapter.

The Capitals

The south transept contains some of the most memorable capitals in the whole cathedral. These, according to Jerry Sampson, may well have been carved as a young man by Adam Lock himself.

At this stage in the building when the capitals first become 'inhabited', the carvings are mainly of people rather than creatures. On the free-standing pillar nearest the south is perhaps the best known set of carvings which tell a story of crime and punishment. It starts at the south-east corner of the capital and moves anti-clockwise. A boy holds a basket of grapes and an adult, looking surreptitiously over his shoulder, plucks another bunch. These are the grape stealers! Moving round to the second image, the thieves have indeed been seen and a vineyard worker with his axe or hoe is indicating their presence with the index finger of his right hand. He is talking to the farmer, easily identified, wearing a large hat and carrying a pitch-fork.

Going round to the third episode, the thief has been caught, still clutching his grapes. The body language of both figures speaks volumes. Finally the punishment is administered to a now very woebegone thief; the farmer is using up so much energy, that his hat slips off the back of his head.

The pillar to the north of this has the biggest and most obvious man with tooth-ache. He is one of several hidden about the capitals. Moving again anti-clockwise is a man pulling a thorn out of his foot. He is known as 'Spinario' and is originally a Greco-Roman figure adopted by masons all over western Europe, wherever gothic architecture is found. On the west side of this capital is a cobbler mending a shoe.

The Font

This stands unusually in the south transept, where it was originally positioned long before the completion of the building but when the door to the present east cloister was used as the principal entrance. Was it left there by sheer inertia as some suggest, or does it significantly bind the old cathedral to the new, as a symbol of continuity? Made of Bath stone, it came from the old building, very close on the south side, and is at least 1000 years old. It is still in use today. Outwardly, the font does not look as Saxon as it once did. It has a Jacobean cover of c.1635. The cover was repainted in 1982 in the style of the period and the bowl inside is lead-lined. The 'drum' of the font (the oldest part) has been much restructured and re-cut, most likely to destroy its apparent Saxon origins and

to make it compatible with its gothic surroundings; a striving for harmony, perhaps? Certainly the eight arches were rather crudely given definite points and the capitals show signs of, at least, reduction. The spandrels while distinctly lacking in detail, nevertheless show signs of foliate sprays, each of which is slightly different. Using other examples of early fonts, it is possible that the rim contained some form of Saxon text. Within each arch there are 'shadows' of long-robed figures, possibly saints or angels, some with evident signs of fixings for a halo. The plinth and step were probably constructed to support the font when it was placed in its present position.

The Glass

The south window by Powell dominates this transept and was placed there in 1905. It depicts 'The River of the Water of Life' as it is described in the book of Revelation. It is a fine example of the Powell workshop. The lower windows (1903) illustrate the Birth, Baptism, Agony, Crucifixion, Resurrection and Ascension of Christ. These traceries are filled with fifteenth century glass, depicting from west to east: a bishop; St Dunstan as archbishop, tweaking the nose of the devil with a pair of tongs; St John the Evangelist holding a cup with a dragon coming out of it; and St John the Baptist holding an Agnus Dei.

The Crossing

The Scissor Arches

The crossing is much altered from its early origins mainly because the existing tower was part of the second build: the expansion and extension of the cathedral. The tower was originally only 43 cm (17 inches) above the nave roof; the relevant stringcourse is obvious on the outside. However, having completed the original build, including the chapter house by 1306, it was decided a few years later, to heighten the tower and extend the whole building by a considerable amount eastwards. In 1313 this process began, concentrating first on raising the tower. Because of the geology, the added weight of the heightened tower, including a cap spire, caused the western pillars of the crossing to bed or sink into the ground beneath. On the east side the ground seems to be rock, but on the west it is probably marl. The pillars sank on the north-west by 8 cm (3 inches), and on the south-west by 10 cm (4 inches), thus causing great tears to appear in the tower structure. The builders should have been alert to potential trouble, since when the short, stumpy tower was built, there was even then, considerable subsidence particularly affecting the nave arcade on the south side. Colchester first drew attention to the pillars before the mid-way

The scissor arches

'break', noticing that they lean away from the crossing. At that time, extra strengthening was given to the nave arches at triforium level, not visible from the ground but still in position in the south nave aisle roof space. With the much increased height after 1313–1322, it is hardly surprising to find the structure in trouble.

Corrective measures in plenty were taken. The arcade arches on both sides immediately to the west of the crossing and those to the north and south had extra shafts added giving an additional 45 cm (18 inches) support. These are obvious from the new designs of the mouldings and capitals, quite different from the stiff-leaf carving and more perpendicular in style. Internal buttresses in the same area were inserted at triforium to clerestory level. High up in the clerestory on both sides of the crossing, partially blocked up windows with this extra buttressing are clearly visible from both transepts, and also in the first nave bay on each side. These probably did most of the work in stabilizing the structure. Two triforium arches on both sides of the nave abutting the crossing were also blocked as further buttressing: all part of the general campaign to stop the tower from collapsing.

Thomas of Whitney, master mason at the start of the proceedings, was succeeded by William Joy, who was certainly responsible for the spectacular scissor arches, built between 1338 and 1348. These have been much discussed as to the degree of weight transference and bracing. Modern opinion seems to be that their effect is not great in terms of structural efficacy but they are a powerful statement of confidence. Whatever the case, there has been no more movement in the structure since. Scissor arches were not unique to Wells. They were used on a smaller scale in the eastern transepts at Salisbury and in Glastonbury Abbey, where now only the springers are visible, rising from the ground. After the Black Death in 1348, and designed by William Joy who is presumed to have perished in the Plague, a very modern-looking grid system was inserted into the tower higher up on the inside, to strengthen and keep straight the lightened outer wall. This was the last measure to be carried out.

The Fan Vaulting
The original intention was of an open tower with light streaming down from above, from louvred windows and a hanging lantern. This was a popular concept at the time and indeed, to this day, beautiful rounded mouldings and shafts, designed to be seen from below, still exist above the present crossing vault. The fan vaulting was added c.1480 and was the work of William Smyth, master mason who was also responsible for the fan vaulting

The Crossing: fan vaulting and organ

in the Stillington Chapel and for the canopy in Dr Sugar's chantry chapel; he was subsequently involved with the nave and transept vaulting of Sherborne Abbey. The work in the crossing came some while after the collapse of the cap spire in 1438, which had been struck by a bolt of lightning. Although the spire was never rebuilt (could God have spoken?) decorative pinnacles in perpendicular style, apart from the original large corner ones, were added to finish off the parapet of the tower. Coupled with these repairs, it was decided to fill in the crossing with the fan vaulting, to prevent often quite strong down-draughts, uncomfortable for those processing into the quire. Enough of an opening was left for a hanging lantern still to give some down-light, nowadays substituted by large electric spot lights.

Right in the centre of the crossing is a circular Maundy Stone, dated 8th April 1993, in Belgian blue marble (a polished limestone) with a surround of York Crossland stone. It commemorates the visit of Her Majesty the Queen and was unveiled by Sir Walter Luttrell, Lord Lieutenant of Somerset. It was designed by the former cathedral architect Alan Rome who also designed the present organ case in 1974 when still in office. The lettering was cut by Leda Kindersley and Eric Morland.

The salamander corbel

The North Transept

Linking the two transepts is the pulpitum, built c.1335, on which the organ has stood ever since. It was substantially modified, by pushing out the central section into the crossing, to accommodate the new Willis organ in the mid-nineteenth century. In the late thirteen hundreds, William Wynford had screened off the eastern aisles, enclosing the chapels to the east and the passage to the chapter house steps to the north. By this time the chapels on the east side may have disappeared or at least been made smaller, to allow for easy access to the chapter house. In their place, now on the east wall, are the tombs of Bishop Still (1593-1608) and Bishop Kidder (1691-1703) and his wife. Bishop Still is splendidly dressed in late Elizabethan style, ready to take up his place in the House of Lords. As he was twice married and had numerous offspring, his tomb is frequently asked for by descendants from all over the world. Bishop Kidder's tomb was erected shortly after the death of his daughter who is shown lying in classical pose pointing heavenwards where she appears to be confident that her parents will be. Bishop Kidder and his wife died in the terrible storm of 1703 when a tall chimney of the palace crashed through the roof onto their bed. On the north wall to the right of the door, is the tomb of Thomas Cornish, who was titular Bishop of Tenos in the Aegean archipelago; during this period he also acted as suffragan bishop of Bath and Wells during the episcopates of Stillington, Fox, King, and Hadrian. In addition he was a canon residentiary and successively chancellor then precentor of the cathedral, prior of St John's Hospital and, among other parishes, vicar of St Cuthbert's in Wells. This tomb has at times been used as an Easter Sepulchre. Once the chapels with their screens were removed, the central triple shaft nearest Wynford's archway on the west side, was left cut off in mid air. Subsequently it was beautifully capped by a delicate and intricate corbel of a lizard or salamander eating fruit.

In the main part of the transept, the most obvious focus is the clock and quarter-jack on the present west wall. This wall was also constructed during Wynford's time specifically to support the clock. It thereby enclosed the present canons' and virgers' vestries. The canons' vestry was the book store before the Bubwith library was built in the mid-fifteenth century. In the very early days, before 1306, the north transept itself had been used from time to time as a temporary chapter house.

The Clock

Before examining the present clock in detail it is worth noting the existence of an earlier time piece associated with Wells, possibly a water clock, although very early mechanical clocks already existed. It was discovered very recently by Robert Dunning when going through an early account roll dated to 1292, exactly one hundred years before the clock of today. The roll is now in the Somerset Heritage Centre in Taunton (SHC DD/CC/B 1280-90). The relevant entry reads; "In cordis ad orliag' per J de Ba' et Robert de Chilham empt' 10s.", 'On ropes for the clock bought by J de Ba' and Robert de Chilham 10s.' It is not known what this clock looked like as this is the first evidence that has come to light.

The present clock is a main attraction for visitors, whatever else they are seeking in the cathedral. It is often described as the second oldest clock in the world and the oldest with its original face. It was certainly in place by 1392/93, when an entry appears in the communar's accounts for the year, paying ten shillings as wages to the keeper of 'la Clokke'. The date normally given for its installation is c.1390. Older by five years or so is the Salisbury clock (without a face) and when Bishop Erghum was translated from Salisbury to Wells in 1388, it is not unreasonable to suppose that he brought his clockmaker with him. Certainly the mechanism appears to have been designed by the same man. The original Wells' works are now in the Science Museum in London, restored and still working. The current mechanism is dated 1880 and was built by Gillett and Bland of Croydon, eminent clockmakers of their time. Until 2010, the clock was hand-wound at least twice a week by several generations of the Fisher family (local to Wells), seven hundred and fifty turns at a time. It has now been mechanised and three electric motors do the work of one man.

The clock face depicts the universe as it appeared to be, before the studies of Copernicus. In the centre is a brown knob with wavy lines round it: the earth. The rings or dials have been used to give the impression that the sun, moon and stars all rotate round the earth. In each corner, not very easy to see, are angels holding the heads of men with puffed-out blowing faces. These are the four winds from the four corners of the earth. Three dials help to tell the time and although last repainted in 1727, still have their medieval appearance. The outer dial shows the hours; two sets of twelve, with midday at the top and midnight at the bottom. Both these are shown as circles filled by a red floriated cross. The sun as a big star is the pointer. Moving inwards, the middle dial marks the minutes with a tiny star. The innermost ring shows the days of the lunar month (the number of days since the new moon), indicated by a trident or a crescent moon with pointer. In the disc, the moon can be seen exactly as it appears in the sky on any particular day. This moon disc is balanced by Phoebe the moon goddess, with a Latin inscription above her: 'Sic peragrat Phoebe', 'thus travels the moon'. Nowadays, at every quarter, jousting knights go round at the top (in medieval times it only happened on the hour), one knight in particular, even after well over six hundred years, being quite incapable of staying on his horse.

At the same time as the jousting knights embark on their performance, the quarter-jack, known as Jack Blandiver, kicks the quarter hours (one ding-dong for each) with his heels. On the hour he bangs the bell in front of him with the hammer held in his right hand. He too has been repainted and even given a costume update but the wood from which he is made is as old as the clock. Above his head is a lever with a wire attached to it which disappears into a hole in the plaster vault. The wire then travels right up the central tower where it pops out of the lead roof and is attached to a large clapper of an equally large bell, in one of the corner pinnacles, so that all of Wells knows what time it is, at the same time as Jack Blandiver bangs his little bell.

Carvings
Underneath the clock is a statue by Estcourt J. Clack of 'Christus Redemptor' (Christ the Redeemer). It was carved in yew wood in 1954 and placed in the cathedral in 1956. It is a depiction of three stages: the crucifixion, the resurrection (the bonds are loose) and Christ ascending. This is where,

during the visitor season, a chaplain says short prayers on the hour, to give time for reflection and peace.

On this wall there are some more capitals deserving of inspection. Left of the clock, on the capital by the north nave aisle, is a man with a large bandage or strap under his nose, linked to his cap (some say it is to ward off the plague), two bird-like dragons with a baboon's head in the middle of them, and a man with foliage placed over his head like a cap. On the right of the clock is Aaron busy writing his name, the first A has been cut off by the corner of the clock face (as has his head) but RON can be seen; Moses holding the stone tablets; and a man writing a scroll with the letters APA visible. In the corner, under Jack Blandiver is a man carrying a goose, and another possible tooth-ache or stroke victim.

Aaron writing his name and Moses with the stone tablets

On the north wall is a canopied memorial, designed by Benjamin Ferrey, to the men of the Somerset Light Infantry who fell in the South African War of 1878-79. The figure of David in the centre, with the fallen giant Goliath behind him, was created by George Tinworth. A small frog looks on. The regimental colours, presented by Prince Albert in 1846, were laid up over this memorial until, in February 1955, they were removed to the Regimental Museum.

The Glass

High up in the clerestory on the east side, almost impossible to view from the ground, is a striking window of the early Renaissance. It was created by Arnold of Nijmegen, a Fleming who had set up a school of glass in Rouen in France. It is dated 1507 and is two thirds of a triptych showing the execution of John the Baptist. The main figure on the right is the executioner about to take a swing and on the left, John the Baptist in magnificent martyr's red, waiting patiently for his head to fall into his ready positioned hands. This window tells a story: above, behind the balustrade on the left are Herod and Herodias with the head of John the Baptist on a platter in front of them. Herodias is pricking the tongue of the Baptist with a bodkin or pin, as she had sworn to silence him. The expression on her face is vicious. On the right are burghers, musicians, and probably the donor dressed in blue at the front, leaning on the balustrade. This window was bought by the Dean and Chapter in 1811-12 during the Napoleonic wars, initially to fill the centre light of the great west window, where its colouring and design were shown to be totally inappropriate. It was subsequently moved to its present and unsatisfactory position.

On the north wall above the War Memorial, the glass was inserted in 1903 by James Powell and Co. It was intended as a memorial to the men of the Somerset Light Infantry and North Somerset Yeomanry who fell in the Boer War. The high level glass is similarly vibrant in colour to that of the south transept and the lower glass was made deliberately different to provide a contrast. The high lancets show angels with Crowns of Life and Palms of Victory in the centre. Beneath are warriors from Abraham and Moses to the Duke of Wellington, a colour-sergeant of the Somerset regiment, and General Gordon. The lower windows depict kings connected to the history of the early church in Somerset: Ina, Egbert, Alfred, Edward the Elder, Athelstan, and Edgar. The arms and badges at the bottom are: the Royal Arms, Bishop Kennion, North Somerset Yeomanry, Somerset Light Infantry, Earl of Cork and Orrery (Lord Lieutenant), and Dean Jex-Blake. It is here, at the end of the north transept, that wreaths are laid and a simple ceremony conducted on 11th November each year to remember all those fallen in war.

Opposite: Arnold of Nijmegen's depiction of the execution of John the Baptist

Sancti Johannis. Decollatio.

The quire before evensong

Chapter 5
The Quire

Coming into the quire from the crossing is to experience a complete change in atmosphere. The great, open, straightforward spaces of the nave and transepts give way to something much more intimate; effectively closed off from the rest of the building, it is warmed by furniture, by light and by colour. It is important also to see it in the evening, at evensong for example, when the lamps are switched on, giving off a soft, diffused light, enhancing this feeling of intimacy. This is indeed the heart of the building, emphasized by what is in fact, with all the doors closed, a small church surrounded by a large one, embracing it on all sides. Here in medieval times all eight regular offices took place, sung by the Vicars Choral, the young clerks who deputized for the canons, and six choir boys known as 'quiristers'. It was the duty of the cathedral canons to sing and pray on behalf of the people; a routine which went on from matins (*media nocte*), at about 2.00 a.m., a short service followed by some rest until 'morrow' mass at dawn. Worship then continued at intervals with offices of varying lengths until compline, the last office of the day, following which, at about 6.00 p.m., the canons and their vicars had supper. The constant round of worship made this space, in medieval thinking, "the gateway to heaven", as it gave the closest possible sense of the presence of the Divine, enhanced by the beauty of the liturgy.

Construction
This is a very complicated space as it has had two major alterations and some smaller ones since the original Early English quire was built. This first quire consisted of only the three western bays, with the crossing and one bay of the nave included in the quire complex. In terms of the building plan

it embraced phases one and two. Work probably started in 1175 and would have entailed a levelling of the site, the digging of the foundations and the construction of a great mortared rubble raft, in the area of the present presbytery (the area between the bishop's throne and the altar rail to the east) up to just beyond the wall behind the high altar of today. This raft was probably deemed necessary because the eastern end of the proposed first construction was close to soggy ground and 'the wells' (springs), found today in the grounds of the bishop's palace.

In 2008, the north quire aisle wall was breached in the fifth bay from the crossing, in order to provide visitor access to the undercroft. Only since then, has it been possible to envisage the eastern end of the first build with some accuracy. Breaching the wall showed, that when the quire was extended in the fourteenth century, the quire aisle outer wall was built on top of the original twelfth century wall; distinctly different mortars had been used and it was evident that the twelfth century wall bench continued right up to Corpus Christi chapel on the north side and St Katherine's chapel on the south. Coupled with evidence of an outer eastern wall, found by master mason W. A. Wheeler in 1968, just to the west of the two retroquire pillars nearest to the quire, it would now appear that the cathedral had a square east end, of the same width as the quire and its aisles. All the evidence was examined by Jerry Sampson and tabled in an as yet unpublished paper (see diagram opposite). This would indicate a central Lady Chapel at the eastern end, probably flanked by two smaller chapels on either side. There is mention of an altar to St Mary Magdalene in 1263. This confirms the similarity to the east end of Winchester Cathedral and St Alban's Abbey. An impressive ambulatory would have linked the eastern chapels with the quire. Most likely, services were held in the eastern Lady Chapel while the quire was still under construction (phase 2) as, on the outer wall of the south quire aisle an outline of a processional door is clearly visible, giving access to the east end. The daily round of worship was thus established from early times.

The second building phase mentioned previously, comprised the erection of the east wall of the quire with its high vault, the three western bays and the eastern arms of the transepts, again with temporary processional doors (see previous chapter). Looking at the pillars to the west of the nineteenth century pulpit and the bishop's seat (cathedra) of c.1340, Wearly examples of stiff leaf foliage carving can be seen on the pillar capitals: very primitive by comparison with the much more elaborate examples further west in the nave. The carvers' skill was evolving over time. Apart from the pillars, most details of the original build are no longer be seen as, between about 1320 and 1340, a major re-construction and extension took place.

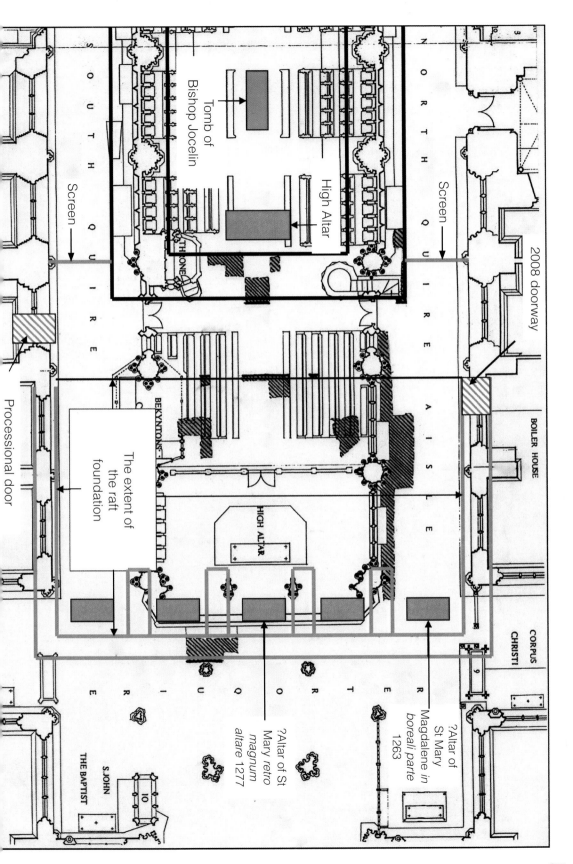

SOUTH QUIRE

NORTH QUIRE

Screen

Screen

Tomb of
Bishop Jocelin

High Altar

THRONE

2008 doorway

BOILER HOUSE

Processional door

BEKYNTON'S

The extent of
the raft
foundation

HIGH ALTAR

AISLE

CORPUS
CHRISTI

?Altar of
St Mary
Magdalene *in
boreali parte*
1263

?Altar of St
Mary *retro
magnum
altare* 1277

THE BAPTIST

S.JOHN

RETROQUIRE

67

The Fourteenth Century Extension

Almost at the same time as the heightening of the central tower, a new Lady Chapel was being constructed to the east of the original outer east wall. This was completed by 1326 so that services could be held there while the quire was being extended by a further three bays. The new east wall of the quire with its high vault comes just to the west of the original outer wall.

The fourteenth century extension, instigated by Bishop Drokensford and master mason Thomas of Whitney, was taken over at the development of the quire by Bishop Ralph of Shrewsbury, Dean John de Godelee and master mason William Joy. At this point (July 1329) Bishop Ralph was only two months into his episcopate. Work must have proceeded apace, as not only was a new quire and presbytery created, having demolished the old wall, chapels and retroquire, but the old three bay quire had to be altered to harmonize with the new structure. The eye had to be deceived into believing that this was one integrated space. Looked at closely, many differences can be seen between the two halves, although they are not immediately apparent.

In the original quire there were two-arch bays at triforium level, very similar to those in the transepts, although slightly wider. Verticality, which remained important in the quire, had been emphasized by the wall shafts from which the vault rises, which start at the string course below the triforium arches, as opposed to the horizontal emphasis which has been observed in the nave. To blend in with the new "tabernacle" decorated style of the eastern bays of the current quire at triforium level, the arches to the west were blocked in (their outline can still be seen within the triforium itself) and overlaid with the new "tabernacle" design. The craftsmanship was not always of the highest standard in this area, since probably the best masons had been pulled away to concentrate on preventing the central tower from collapsing. This can also be seen in the clerestory windows, where the attempt to emulate the new style of the presbytery, was rather primitive.

Perhaps the most powerful feeling of harmony is created by the re-construction of the vault, with its design very much associated with William Joy. The high vault of the three western bays, would originally have been ribbed, as in the nave. The present continuous vault is often described as 'lierne' but is in fact a basic barrel or tunnel vault with 'lierne' attributes (Sampson). There is an almost identical vault in the collegiate church of Ottery St Mary, also attributed to Joy.

Opposite: William Joy's decorated vault

Two things cannot be masked; the pillars are clearly different in design, the watershed being at the bishop's seat on the south side and the nineteenth century pulpit on the north. The new design has very different capitals and purbeck marble stone shafts by way of contrasting colour. The two slim pillars right at the east end behind the high altar have a blue lias core with purbeck shafts as have the first two slim pillars in the retroquire. By this time purbeck marble had almost completely superseded the use of blue lias. Secondly, looking up to clerestory level, the windows within the two halves are also at different levels. It was during this time c.1335 that the present pulpitum, at that stage a stone screen straight across, was built to finish off the work at the western end.

Misericords
The entire new build of the fourteenth century was completed by c.1340. To celebrate and beautify this space, some significant touches were added. In the first instance, new canons' stalls were ordered (1325/26), complete with misericords, still in place under the re-constructed seats in the present day quire. The canons were ordered to pay for their own stall at a cost of 30 'solidi' each. By the time the seats were installed in the quire (c.1335), there was still a debt of about £200 and a fund raising drive was instigated, directed to the prebendaries (canons) who had failed to make a contribution (C.M. Church). At this stage the boy choristers sat on benches in front of the stalls.

Original misericord of 1335

Misericords were created to alleviate the tiredness of the clergy and their vicars, obliged to stand for long periods during the offices of which there were at least eight a day. The misericords were ledges underneath the hinged seats on which the vicars or prebendaries could perch, while still appearing, in their long robes, to be standing. The semblance of respect to God was paramount. The pity or mercy (misericordia) was to the legs! The interest of the misericords lies in their carvings of diverse themes and patterns, similar to those of the stone capitals, each an individual creation. Sixty five misericords remain and one is always on show in the quire. Three others are on display at the south entrance to the retroquire and one is on permanent loan to the Victoria and Albert Museum in London. These four were displaced when the seating was re-arranged in the mid nineteenth century. It is possible to see photographs of all the misericords in a booklet in the library, by request.

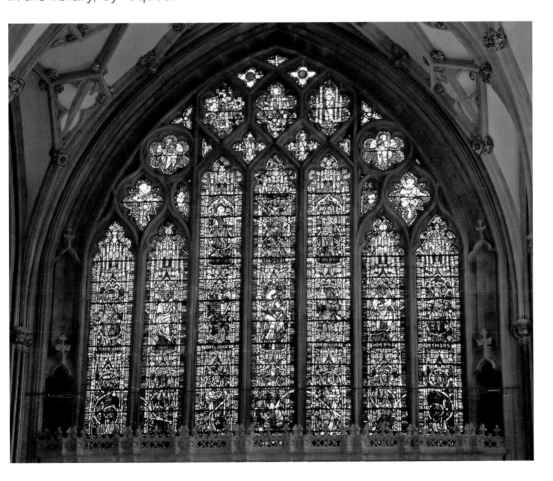

The Glass
The final embellishments of the quire were both installed c.1340, to celebrate its completion. The bishop's seat (cathedra) gave full authority and weight to the cathedral church. The crowning glory however, was the great Jesse window (above) at the eastern end, above the high altar.

It has been said that it is like a reredos for the high altar, even though it is far above. This also points to a connection between the west front and its Christ in Judgment and Glory at the centre, although this window also depicts the genealogy of Christ. The most important section is the centre: three tall lights with traceries which give significance to the whole window.

Looking at the centre light, at the bottom is the reclining figure of Jesse (father of King David) with his bearded face supported on his arm on the left. Out of his side, points of white glass can be seen emerging, the root of a vine, with branches issuing from it, winding round all the figures in the window. Above Jesse is the Virgin with the Child on her knee. Above, is the crucified Christ on a T-shaped cross of vivid green. It grows directly out of the main stem of Jesse's vine, and the green of the cross connects it to the concept of the Tree of Life. Above, but now almost non-existent as most of the original glass has fallen out, is Christ in Majesty or Christ as Judge, echoing the west front, with the traceries on either side depicting people emerging from their tombs, again echoing the west front, at crucifixion level, and above them on either end are angels with trumpets. In between the angels, on the left is a king rising from his tomb and on the right, a bishop. High in the apex is the dove, the Holy Spirit with, just below on the left, the sun and, on the right, the moon. The other main figures in the window are from Christ's genealogy as described in Matthew Chapter 1, with the addition of two prophets, Ezekiel and Daniel. Again, those close to the centre are the most significant, as for example on the second level from the bottom, left of the Virgin and Child, is King David with his harp and on the right is David's son King Solomon, holding the temple of Jerusalem, which he built, in his hand. On close inspection, the temple looks more like a

Gothic church, familiar of course, to the glass painters who had no idea what the original temple looked like. Above David is Mary again, as an

older, grieving woman, flanking the crucified Christ, with John the beloved disciple on the right, reflecting the Rood figures on the nave scissor arch.

Apart from the detail and complexity, it is the colour which draws people in. Not for nothing is it often referred to as 'the golden window', for its predominance of deep yellow silver stain and green, with vivid splashes of ruby red. It is the lack of much blue colouring which sets it apart. Facing east with the rising sun on a bright morning, it is truly spectacular. Christ, the light of the world is there!

This window is one of the best preserved of its period, perhaps the finest example in England and even in relation to the best fourteenth century glass in the rest of western Europe. Because of its historical importance, much care has been taken to conserve it. One major intervention was that of taking the window down during the Second World War and storing it in the small triforium chamber in the south transept. It was re-assembled and put back in its place in 1945. Then in 2010, extensive conservation commenced, as bowing lead had caused damp and therefore dirt and corrosion to penetrate the interior of the glass. Isothermal (secondary) glazing was inserted in panels on the outside to protect against the weather, and partial re-leading, cleaning and fixing of paint was carried out on the inside, by the local firm of Holywell Glass (headed by director, Stephen Clare), specialists in medieval glass conservation. Vigorous fund raising by the Friends of the cathedral, kick-started the campaign to raise the necessary £500,000.

Looking up to clerestory level on each side of the Jesse Window, two further contemporary medieval windows can be seen, designed to be read in conjunction with the east window. All four have representations of kings or saints, as support for the Judgement, similar again to the ideas incorporated in the west front. The two windows on the south side were re-leaded during 1991-93 and those on the north also need attention. On the north side, reading from the east, are (a pope), St George and St Blaise; in the second window, St Gregory, St Giles and St Richard of Chichester who had only been canonized in 1262. On the south side, starting nearest to the east are St Clement, St Oswald? and St Ethelbert; the second window has St Brice, St Ambrose and (a bishop). Originally there were two other windows, one on each side, probably lost in the seventeenth century.

What a powerful aid and focus these east end windows must have been to the liturgy, daily taking place around the high altar. Not only can the importance of Christ's ancestry, right down from Abraham, be understood but in the centre section of the Jesse window is a potent statement of faith, from the Incarnation, through the Crucifixion and the Resurrection to the gift of the Holy Spirit for all time.

The Victorian Restoration

Minor changes took place in the following centuries as, for example, the gift of a new organ, given by Dean Robert Creyghtone after the Restoration of 1660. This was to last for almost 200 years. During this period, between 1663-4, various prebendal stalls which had been smashed during the time of the Commonwealth were restored. Each prebendary had to pay £2 2s. 0d to repair their own particular stall. Creyghtone also gave £300 towards bookcases and other library furniture and for "many valuable books" (C.M. Church). In the 1680s, new wooden galleries were erected over the prebendal stalls, for families of 'quality' and "ye Bishops' deans' and canons' wifes" (chapter minutes). This necessitated the canopies of the old stalls being ruthlessly truncated, to make way for the new construction. The galleries were approached by stairs from behind the pillars in the quire aisles.

By the time Edmond Goodenough (1831-45) became dean, the whole building needed attention, including the quire. It was Dean Goodenough who removed the monuments to the cloisters and commenced the so-called 'great scrape' of 1842-44, to remove the white or ochre lime-wash from the stone. This was overseen by the architect Benjamin Ferrey. It was Anthony Salvin however, who was appointed specifically to attend to the restoration of the quire when Dean Richard Jenkyns (1845-54) succeeded Dean Goodenough. The wooden galleries were demolished as they were by then not very safe and the staircases were somewhat rickety and also blocked the quire aisles. Because more seating was required by then, Salvin built new prebendal stalls further back between the arches with stone canopies over, using a design imitating the fourteenth century style. The original stalls had therefore to be moved forward and altered. The boy choristers, originally perched on benches, were given a row of seats on both sides, in front of the men. All lime-wash was removed including the vault where the plaster fields were repainted and the bosses, coloured and gilded. The reason for all this was described by Canon Barnard (before 1843) "….. an unbroken mass of white-wash and yellow ochre…..the fine sculpture of the capitals were scarcely to be distinguished. The choir [sic] at this time was fitted with very plain oak stalls, with canopies running in a line in front of the arches destroying their proportions, and hiding the columns and capitals".

Salvin's prebendal stalls

At the sanctuary end a pavement of Minton tiles was laid, as was the case in the Lady Chapel, and on each side, the third clerestory windows counting from the east were re-glazed, the original medieval glass having been lost. On the north, the window designed by Joseph Bell of Bristol was installed in 1851. The colours are wholly incompatible with those of

the medieval glass. On the south, the window shows St Patrick, St Dunstan, and St Benignus. Installed in 1846, it was designed by Thomas Willement, who was also responsible for the restoration of the east window of the Lady Chapel.

At Whitsun 1847, after a lapse of over a century, processing was re-introduced into the quire, in an attempt to give more dignity to the proceedings. Mention has been made (Colchester) of an original bow-fronted throne, the cathedra, truncated to allow for more processional space. However, recent in-depth examination of the throne has been carried out by Andrew Budge from which it would appear that there is no evidence of an alteration in the structural shape at the front. Salvin did make several repairs and alterations, using Doulting stone in what is predominantly a throne constructed in Bath stone by the master mason William Joy. He moved the stone access door from the west side of the cathedra to the east, giving the bishop more space to take his seat. Also clearly visible is paler Bath stone used to heighten the crenellations on either side, presumably when the original decorative pinnacles topping them were removed. Canon Barnard described the stone as being painted to look like green marble with a landscape at the back (probably eighteenth century). This was laboriously scraped off. Opposite the cathedra is the nineteenth century pulpit, designed by Salvin and paid for by Dean Jenkyns and his wife. Also put in place was a new Willis organ, so large that Salvin was obliged to push out the centre section of the stone pulpitum to accommodate the pipes. The opening recital on the new organ was given on 2nd June 1857. Costs for all this work were a constant source of worry and in the quire alone, came to £4,694 8s. 9d. Despite generous gifts, such as that of £1,000 from Dean Jenkyns himself, a temporary loan had to be negotiated.

Further Developments
The Embroideries

The stall banners in particular, but also all the cushions and backs, give a welcome warmth to the general atmosphere of the quire. They were executed in the period between 1937 and 1952; a large proportion during the Second World War. Alice, Lady Hylton designed the needlework and gathered together about a hundred embroiderers of whom seven were men. Dean Malden (1933-50) chaired a committee, formed to co-ordinate the work and it was he originally who, impressed by the embroideries at Winchester Cathedral, planted the germ of an idea to enhance the quire at Wells. He was aided by the architect, Sir Charles Nicholson who suggested covering the backs of the stalls with decorative banners.

Spread over all the seats is a wealth of design and detail, ranging from myth and legend, kings and bishops, to organists, ancient music notation and illuminated manuscripts. The bishop's seat is embellished with, appropriately, a jewelled embroidery of St Andrew, patron saint of the cathedral. Looking at the stall banners, there are five with gold backgrounds to denote the five canons (the quinque), who in medieval times formed the administrative chapter: the dean, precentor, chancellor treasurer and archdeacon of Wells. All the others have backgrounds alternating red and blue. They contain designs representing a selection of bishops through the ages, depicted in anti-clockwise direction, starting next to the dean's stall with Bishop John Drokensford (1309-29), right round to Bishop Wynne Willson (1921-37), next to the precentor's stall. All have coats of arms, names and dates and stories of their time, or particular interests of an individual bishop. All have mitres except two, who are distinguished by cardinal's hats, namely Hadrian de Costello and Thomas Wolsey. This great enterprise still enthuses even those with no particular needlework skills, by the sheer variety of theme, colour and stitches, so beautifully executed.

The Millennium Altar Frontals

To celebrate the Millennium, new altar frontals and vestments were designed and made, to represent the liturgical colours of each season of the church calendar. Those for the nave altar were designed by Maurice Strike and for the high altar by Jane Lemon. The high altar work was carried out by the Royal School of Needlework at Hampton Court and the nave altar work by the Sarum Group of Embroiderers, in Jane Lemon's workshop near Salisbury. All were funded by private subscription. It was an attempt by the Chapter to place worship and the meaning of the liturgy in a modern context; it was

Easter high altar frontal

given the title 'Mystery and Meaning'. Altogether there are sixty three pieces, in which the overriding theme is light and symbol, bringing out in textiles the link with the soaring vaults of the building and the colour of the stained glass. The designs of the nave altar are intentionally diffuse, as in the inception of an idea, and those of the high altar are strong, clear and often three-dimensional: the affirmation.

Presbytery Seating

The present seating was installed during the time of Dean Armitage Robinson (1911-33). It was most probably one of his first improvements to the general well-being of the quire. Stylistically the seats belong to the early twentieth century. They are generally of good plain workmanship but enhanced by some fine figurehead carvings on the top of the bench ends. These range from kings and bishops to a doctor of law and possibly a woman wearing a scold's bridle.

Quire Sedilia (clergy seats for the mass)

Later still, cushions and backs for the sedilia were upholstered and embroidered to celebrate the Golden Jubilee of Queen Elizabeth II in 2002. The designs reflect the Victorian pavement in the sanctuary. They were conceived by Nancy Long and carried out by members of the cathedral embroidery group, including the then dean, Richard Lewis. The centre seat features in gold, 'E II R 1952 – 2002' and was shown to the queen when she came to visit during her tour of the country. As with the quire stall embroideries, the Friends of the cathedral were deeply involved in providing the necessary funds.

Altar Rails

The division between the sanctuary and the rest of the quire is indicated by the altar rails. These in the nineteenth century were of elaborately designed brass, which gave way to a simpler design in wood, by Stephen Dykes

Bower (architect) in 1952. Public subscription was again used for this, to commemorate the life of Dean Malden who died in 1950 and was deeply involved in creating the present ambience in the quire.

The Organ

After the considerable alteration of the pulpitum when the new Willis organ was installed, it had no real case, apart from a base and was regarded as ugly by contemporaries. The organ was re-constituted in 1910 by Harrison and Harrison of Durham, who also carried out a comprehensive rebuild in 1973-74.This gave Alan Rome, the then cathedral architect, the initiative to design a new organ case (1974 - pictured below), decorated with two gilded angels on the quire side, out of an original four. One of those remaining can be seen on display in the undercroft, and the other in Wells Museum. Again the Friends made a special drive to produce funds.

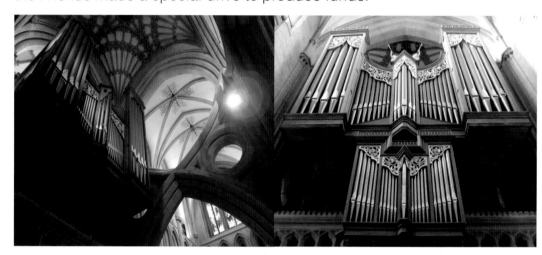

The East End Statues

As far as is known, the niches now containing the statues beneath the Jesse window had long been empty. This does not mean, however, that they were never filled. Free standing statues in such protected places were quite common, and therefore no trace of fixing would have been visible if they had been destroyed. Whatever the case, in the period bridging the First World War, the present statues (right) were erected. Of these, the central figures of the seated Christ, together with St Peter, on the left of Christ and St Andrew on the right, were carried out before 1914 by A. G. Walker and given by Mrs Jessie Head in memory of her brother Douglas McLean. After 1918, the two figures at the far left, St Dunstan and St Patrick were carved by E. C. Burton and again given by Mrs Jessie Head. On the far right, also after 1918, the figures of St David and St George were again carved by Burton but given by the Somerset Freemasons in memory of their brothers who died during the First World War.

South quire aisle through William Wynford's archway

Chapter 6
The Quire Aisles and East End

Construction

Both the quire aisles and the linking east end retroquire form an imposing processional way created in the first half of the fourteenth century. Originally, the aisles at the western end (three bays) were part of the first quire and have been altered to blend with the new work of the 1300s. Looking at the vault, the design is quite clearly attributable to William Joy and is similar to his decorated quire vault. On close examination, the outer walls of the three western bays are thicker than further east; easily shown in the different thickness of the sills under the windows. The new, thinner walls were built on top of twelfth century bases, up to St Katherine's chapel on the south side and Corpus Christi chapel on the north. On both sides east of this line (the east end of the original cathedral) the design of the vault changes as it leads into the retroquire and the eastern chapels. This eastern arm was the work of Thomas of Witney who preceded William Joy and also worked at Exeter, where a similar vault can be seen.

South Quire Aisle

Entering the south quire aisle from the south transept, the processional way stretches into the distance ahead, culminating in the chapel of St John the Baptist at the far end. It contains the tombs of many bishops stretching over the centuries.

The Saxon Bishops

On the left, the side nearest the quire, are effigies of three Saxon bishops whose bones were brought in from the old cathedral and originally given pride of place in the new early Gothic quire. These stone chests are part of a collection of seven, situated in both quire aisles, four on the south side and three on the north. The seven effigies can be divided into two distinct groups. The ones at the western end in both aisles, five in all, were carved in the early English style, dated c.1200. The two at the eastern end, Dudoc on the south side and Giso on the north, were not carved until c.1230 (Rodwell). These two have low mitres of the Anglo-Saxon period and were made deliberately archaic to fit their antiquity. It is fairly certain that this pair, the last two of the Saxon bishops, are accurately named and that the effigies were possibly copied from their original Anglo-Saxon ones. What is less certain is the identity of the other five. In 1979, the wooden boxes inside the stone chests were opened and examined in detail by a pathologist. Mixed up bones were sorted out into individual skeletal remains but it was not possible to determine exactly which bishop was in each chest, even though four had lead name plates. In the nineteenth century the Saxon bishops were removed to the undercroft (a tidying up process of the period) but in 1913 Dean Armitage Robinson moved them to their present position, as close to the quire as possible: a position of honour to emphasize their sanctity and the permanent connection between the early cathedral and the new.

Giso: last bishop of the Saxon cathedral (1061-1088)

Bishop John Harewell 1367-1386

At the south side of the aisle furthest west is the tomb of Bishop Harewell. The effigy is of alabaster and was originally painted. Traces of red can be seen in the folds of his cloak and under his arm. The effigy is most remarkable for the graffiti; the earliest so far noted is of 1625 and much of it is from the seventeenth and eighteenth centuries. More modern additions are not encouraged! Bishop Harewell's feet are resting upon an image of his name (a rebus): two hares drinking from a ribbon-like representation of the rising water of a well. His considerable contribution to the welfare and development of the cathedral was to provide two thirds of the money for the south-west tower and a gift of two bells, the Great Harewell and the Little Harewell. The present tenor bell still bears his name. It has been re-cast several times including the use of the metal from Little Harewell, to strengthen it. The tenor bell weighs 56¼ cwt and Wells is reputed to have the heaviest ring of ten bells in the world. Appropriately the bells are hung in the south-west tower which bears his name.

Bishop Harewell's rebus

Bishop William Bytton II 1267-1274

Bishop Bytton's earthly remains lie on the north side of the aisle, under a blue lias slab which is protected by a Perspex cover. It is thought to be one of the earliest incised tomb slabs in England. According to legend, his skull still contains a perfect set of teeth and his tomb was a focus for tooth-ache sufferers in the Middle Ages, who believed in the healing powers of touching the slab. This may account for the damage that is visible at the head end of the stone.

Bishop George Hooper 1703-1727

Next to Bishop Bytton's ledger stone, inserted in the floor, is that of Bishop George Hooper's wife, and next to her lies the Bishop. Both floor slabs are noteworthy as they display, side by side, two commonly used local stones in the cathedral. Bishop Hooper's is one of the few in Purbeck marble, whereas his wife's is in blue lias. Bishop Hooper was a great scholar, and proficient in Ancient Greek and Latin, Hebrew and Arabic. He left so many books to the cathedral library that three new book presses had to be built to accommodate them.

Bishop Lord Arthur Hervey 1869-1894

This lavish Victorian tomb is made from different types of marble. His effigy is of Carrara marble from Italy. The sarcophagus is made from Derbyshire pink alabaster and the base of Italian Griotte (cherry red) marble. At the feet of the bishop is an ounce or snow leopard which children love to stroke.

Bishop Thomas Bekynton 1443-1465

Proceeding towards the east and passing the south entrance to the quire presbytery, it is worth noting the door and particularly the hinges which date from c.1340, contemporary with the completion of the extended quire. The hinges are a typical local design of the period and continued to be used in Somerset until the 1500s. There are comparable hinges on the north side.

Bekynton's tomb is within his chantry chapel, surrounded with iron railings made locally c.1450. On close inspection there are many small and rather worn heads adorning the iron work and one larger one of a bishop and a number of shields which would have been painted. A legend exists that the Devil feared iron and that was why the chantry was so enclosed. The effigy is of painted alabaster; the paint has been renewed from time to time, the most recent being the restoration of the canopy colouring by Maurice Keevil in 1948. The canopy itself, very intricately and powerfully carved, had been removed during the mid-nineteenth century 'tidy-up' to

Bishop Bekynton's 'Transi' tomb

St Calixtus's chapel at the same time as the removal of the Saxon bishops. It was restored to its proper place by Dean Armitage Robinson in 1922.

This type of tomb, known as a 'Transi' tomb but in layman's terms more often as a 'Memento Mori' (remember you must die), is more common in mainland Europe than in England. Indeed it is possible that Bekynton first noticed them on one of his embassies to France during the Hundred Years War. His friend and patron Archbishop Chichele is reputed to be the first to have a 'Transi' tomb in England and it is possible that Bekynton may have followed him in having his own tomb constructed. Whatever the case, he was obviously impressed by the idea of showing himself on the top level, recumbent in sumptuous robes and as a cadaver in the throes of death underneath, since he had his tomb and chantry constructed fifteen years before his death. Interestingly his face must resemble his likeness at about the age of sixty. The meaning of this type of tomb must have pleased him since it shows that however rich and powerful a person may be in life, in the hour of death all are equal in the sight of God.

Bekynton was a man of vigour and action and often thoughtful towards those in his care. A man of international stature, he had benefited when young from the patronage and protection of Humphrey Duke of Gloucester, and of Henry Chichele, archbishop of Canterbury. His career in the government of the Church gave him entry into all manner of situations, including several diplomatic missions to France. He became trusted secretary to the last Lancaster king, Henry VI and subsequently Lord Privy Seal. Rewarded with the bishopric of Bath and Wells in 1443 he proved a great benefactor to the diocese and its people. Close to home he gave the College of Vicars Choral a new updated charter based on that of Bishop Ralph of Shrewsbury. He also endorsed and amplified a set of rules for the boy choristers and their treatment, ranging from how they should be taught, "…not obscure, but short and concise, for if a teacher is too long-winded, the pupil will become bored…", to detailed instruction for the boys' table manners, "…they must cut their bread or break it decently, not gnaw it with their teeth or tear it with their nails".

Above all, Bekynton was a great builder both in the service of Henry VI where he was involved with the building of Eton College, King's College Cambridge and with a fellow bishop, with the founding of Lincoln College Oxford. In Wells he is remembered for all four gates which surround the cathedral precincts; either his rebus (a beacon and a tun) or his coat of arms, or both, are to be found on them as evidence of his involvement. In addition, several new houses ('new works') were built; twelve on the north

Beckynton's rebus above Penniless Porch

side of the market place and three in Sadler Street. He also added a north wing to the bishop's palace, where the present bishop lives and works. Perhaps his greatest gift to the city was that of ducting water through an underground conduit, from the 'wells' (springs) in the palace gardens, underneath the cathedral cloisters and out into the marketplace, to the site of the present fountain which replaced the original c.1799, so giving all citizens access to pure drinking water. For all his benefactions to the city he is remembered to the present time at a special commemorative evensong of thanksgiving, on the Sunday nearest to the anniversary of his death on 14th January 1465. This is attended by the mayor and all the town council and a posy of flowers is placed by them on the altar of his chantry chapel.

On the aisle vault near Bekynton's tomb are two bosses of particular note. The central boss on a level with the middle of the tomb has the Risen Christ, hand raised in blessing, surrounded by the symbols of the four evangelists: the winged man of St Matthew, the winged lion of St Mark, the winged ox of St Luke and the eagle of St John. At the south-east corner, near the canopy is a curled up dog, being attacked by two fierce rabbits.

Post-restoration replacement misericord (Spinario)

Past Bekynton's tomb at the south-east corner of the inner wall are three misericords, displaced during the mid-nineteenth century restoration. The upper two are original, c.1335, and show at the top Alexander the Great being carried to the skies by two griffins and underneath a dragon or wyvern slayer, thrusting a spear down the gullet of the beast with his left hand. The bottom misericord is a replacement of the 1660s, after the destruction during the Commonwealth period. This shows in wood another portrayal of 'spinario', the man pulling a thorn out of his foot, rather awkwardly placed, wedged underneath the ledge of the misericord.

On the outer wall there are more examples of millennium altar frontals on display, already referred to in the previous chapter.

The Glass

Most of the remaining painted glass in the south quire aisle dates from the early fourteenth century, the period when the quire was extended and the present east end built. The main lights are largely composed of plain diamond quarries, but it is worth looking up at the traceries. Starting at the west end of the aisle, the first top tracery light features an incomplete Coronation of the Virgin with underneath, to the right and left, two censing angels facing towards the centre. In this window the upper part of the westernmost main light is filled with delicate grisaille work which, according to Colchester, probably existed in all the main windows to let in more light.

Proceeding eastwards, in the second window there is a fine portrayal of the Crucifixion in the top tracery, again with a green cross to symbolize the Tree of Life. On the left, kneeling, is the donor with a Latin scroll issuing from him saying, "May the passion of Jesus Christ be our salvation and protection". In the third window the main lights are filled with later heraldic glass of the fifteenth to seventeenth centuries. At the bottom are seven biblical story-telling panels of seventeenth century Flemish origin. Four of the panels depict scenes in the life of Abraham and the other three illustrate the parable of the Unmerciful Servant (Matthew 18: 23-25). These panels were probably meant for domestic purposes and may well have come from a canonical house. The two heraldic shields on either side of the single Flemish panel are on the left the arms of Bishop Bekynton (fifteenth century) and on the right an early representation of the arms of the Dean and Chapter. The top panel in the centre light is the badge of King Richard II from the late fourteenth century, depicting his emblem: a white hart around whose neck is a collar and chain. In the top tracery light is the shield of the See of Bath and Wells (late fourteenth/early fifteenth century). Much of the glass in this window was assembled from other parts of the cathedral.

In the fourth window from the west in the top tracery, is a delicate and tender representation of the Virgin and Child. The Virgin is both crowned and haloed and the Child on her knee is touching her chin with his right hand and holding a small bird in his left. Mother and Child are looking at each other (1330-35). Below this image are two censing angels on the right and left, both angels are facing towards the Virgin and Child, swinging a censer in their right hand and holding an incense boat in the left (1330-35). There is a small section of a canopy in the

main central light, which may have been moved from elsewhere.

The fifth and final window to the east has a depiction of St Michael in the top tracery. He is spearing a dragon at his feet with his right hand and has a shield by his left side.

St Katherine's Chapel
From the south quire aisle, where the early medieval wall bench comes to an end, is the entrance on the south side to St Katherine's chapel. This has many similarities to the corresponding chapel of Corpus Christi on the north side. Both were built as part of the eastern arm of five chapels, under the direction of Thomas of Witney, who had worked at Winchester. He was at that time living and working in Exeter cathedral but combining this with necessary visits to Wells. Corpus Christi and St Katherine's were completed by 1328 and 1329 respectively, at about the time when William Joy replaced Thomas of Witney (c.1327) as master mason; by then Witney was over sixty. In 2003/4 dendrochronology (tree-ring dating) was carried out on the roof timbers of St Katherine's chapel, giving a tree felling date of c.1325 which would confirm satisfactorily the date of the chapel.

The central boss of this chapel vault has been wrongly described as a Katherine wheel, which would of course have been appropriate until it is compared with the almost identical boss in Corpus Christi chapel. The only difference is that there are nine small heads (three in the centre and six round the outside) on the boss in St Katherine's, elsewhere described as a group of virgins, except that three are definitely bearded!

St Katherine's chapel central boss

This chapel is dedicated to Justice and Peace and, as a symbol, the Amnesty candle burns by the south wall with a prisoner of conscience named each month to represent all victims of injustice in prayer. This candle stands on the tomb of Dean John Gunthorpe (1472-98), a man of action who built a whole wing on the Deanery. His rebus of a cannon or gun can be seen on the outside of the structure. On the top edge of the tomb, on the right, an iron bar runs along, once thought to have held prickets for candles, lit before a fifteenth century Nativity scene. A modern sculpture placed on the tomb in 2011 is of an agonized face in Sicilian marble behind metal bars, entitled 'A Second Home'; it is the work of Simon Burns-Cox.

On the west wall under the window is a delicately engraved brass plaque of the seventeenth century in memory of Humphrey Willis who died in 1618. Fascinating detail reveals a whole pictorial list of his hobbies and a depiction of the 'whole armour of God' (Ephesians 6) and in the top left hand corner are four Hebrew letters engraved on a sun: the Tetragrammaton. These four letters are the name of God. The Latin inscription has been translated by Mr Justice Coleridge, and can be seen to the right.

Above the altar on the east wall is a reredos (below) made up of fragments of late perpendicular design; part of the remains of the front of the wooden galleries in the quire, salvaged during the nineteenth century restoration and already mentioned in the previous chapter. In the centre of the reredos is a heavily gilded Flemish carving of the late seventeenth century showing, from left to right, the betrayal of Christ in the Garden of Gethsemane, the Crucifixion in the centre and the Harrowing of Hell on the right, in which Christ is shown, leading the souls of those who were worthy to be saved after Christ's Redemption, out of the mouth of Hell.

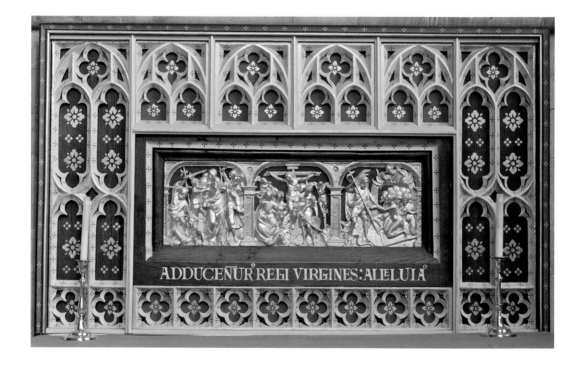

The Glass
The west window contains late fifteenth century diamond quarries in grisaille, portraying flowers and birds of all kinds, probably collected from different parts of the cathedral or from canonical houses to fill this space. The work is very delicate and worth close inspection. The variety in the bird designs

is remarkable including a spoonbill bending over a chest of coins, a peacock, a swan, a bird with a covered cup, and many more.

The south window is filled with glass from Rouen, of Flemish design quite different in style from anything produced in England. This glass was originally acquired to fill the centre light of the great west window; being totally unsuitable in colour and style for that space, it was removed in 1926 and placed in the chapel in 1931.

The three lights to the left probably came from the church of St John the Evangelist in Rouen and illustrate the life of St John as told in 'The Golden Legend'. Two further lights in this series, having travelled to America, returned to England and were bought by the Friends of Wells Cathedral and placed in the east window in 1956. There are three other lights in this series in the Burrell Collection in Glasgow. They are thought to be by a pupil of the Flemish master glazier Arnold of Nijmegen whose school was in Rouen, already mentioned in chapter four. The right hand light of the south window (pictured) depicts St John asleep, seeing as in a dream the seven golden candlesticks and the Emperor Domitian portrayed as Antichrist. This light may have been the work of Arnold of Nijmegen himself. The influence of the German Albrecht Dürer is evident, and it is known that a friendship and exchange of creative ideas existed between Dürer and Arnold of Nijmegen.

In the east window are two ovals of French sixteenth century glass, acquired by the Friends of Wells Cathedral. As glass is normally read from the bottom, Joseph should have come before Pilate (Colchester).

Tomb of Bishop John Drokensford (Droxford) 1309 – 1329
Leaving the chapel and turning towards the east, this tomb forms a wall dividing the chapel from the retroquire. Drokensford was bishop during the early part of the extension eastwards and he appropriately lies within the eastern arm which he helped to create. It was also during his episcopate

that the power of the bishop inside the cathedral was curtailed in favour of the Dean and Chapter (1321).

The tomb itself is thought to have some original paint; it also had a high canopy overhead which was removed in 1758 as it was considered to be unsafe. His tomb consists of four types of stone, all to be found in the building as a whole. The effigy and the tomb chest are of Bath stone, the slab on which the effigy rests is of Purbeck marble, the chest platform is blue lias, and the base of the tomb is Doulting stone.

St John the Baptist Chapel

Entering the chapel of St John the Baptist, in the south-east corner of the east wall, it is immediately apparent that the reredos, like that of St Katherine's, is made up of the same wooden tracery, formerly part of the quire galleries. This was assembled by Sir Charles Nicholson, the then cathedral architect. Facing the altar, on the left is a fine tomb, early fourteenth century with an impressive canopy. It is still not known, after much speculation, whose tomb this was although surely that of a person of some eminence.

This chapel houses, in its south-east corner, figures of Joseph, the Virgin Mary and the Christ Child, carved by Estcourt J. Clack out of Sycamore wood in the 1950s. It provides focus for prayer and it is in this chapel that many visitors leave personal prayers, placed on a board provided. A selection of these prayers always forms part of the intercessions of Friday evensong.

The Glass

Most of the glass is fragments of the early 1300s. In the top tracery of the east window, still relatively intact is the figure of Christ, his left arm raised in blessing and holding a book in his right hand. According to Tim Ayers it is part of a Coronation of the Virgin. The fragmented glass in the main lights spans the fourteenth and fifteenth centuries. Again, some of the canopy work is still in situ. In the right hand main light, in the middle panel below the canopy, is a Katherine wheel in white glass.

The south window at the top has the figure of Christ Enthroned, with his right hand raised in blessing and his left hand placed on an orb. Immediately below to the right and left are the remnants of two censing angels. The bottom row of tracery in quatrefoils has, reading from left to right, the heads of St Linus and St Aldhelm, both bearded, St Erkenwald and a pope. These are early fourteenth century and similar to some of the heads in the traceries of the Lady Chapel. In the middle of the main lights is a square panel showing the risen Christ portraying his wounds with an angel bearing a sword on the left. The style is Renaissance and the origin undoubtedly French. It bears the date 1542, which would confirm this (Ayers).

The Cope Chest

This forms a north wall to St John the Baptist chapel. The cope chest is believed to be the oldest dated piece of furniture in England; it was examined in 2003 by the Oxford University Dendrochronology Laboratory.

This confirmed that it was made of local oak, felled c.1120. Even though this is an average dating (ten years on either side is the span) it makes this chest older than the cathedral in which it now stands and therefore it must have come from the Saxon/Norman cathedral to the south. It was treated and tidied up by Donal Channer, a conservation carpenter, in 2007/2008, there having been some poor patching work carried out in the nineteenth and early twentieth centuries. It contains several copes and mass vestments including a seventeenth century fiddle-back and various small articles from the past with interesting embroidery. It is still constantly in use as it is also a storing place for the different coloured separate corner pieces for the millennium altar frontals, which are changed according to the seasons and days of the church calendar.

Cope chest with 14th century canopy and St John the Baptist chapel in the background

The Lady Chapel
Built as the ultimate eastern point of the cathedral, entering the Lady Chapel by way of the three open arches at its west end is to come into a very special space. Partly this feeling is created by the architecture itself: the elongated octagon, the magnificent star vault, its great windows on five sides; and partly also by its dedication to the Virgin Mary at a period when the worship of Mary as the major intercessor in prayer was at its height. It is perhaps difficult to imagine in the present age how sumptuous this chapel would have been in medieval times, after the considerable destruction which occurred in the seventeenth century and the restoration and alterations of the nineteenth.

Construction
It is known that the Lady Chapel was complete by 1326, as it was described in that year as being newly built. Work certainly did not start before the completion of the chapter house in 1306 and may well have been constructed during part of the period when the central tower was raised. The master mason, or architect was almost certainly Thomas of Witney although there is scant documentary evidence, except in one or two cases where reference is made to 'Thomas le Masun'.

Thomas of Witney at the turn of the thirteenth century was already an architect of repute, having a controlling hand at Winchester and Exeter, where he was apparently living for the most part during the building of the Lady Chapel at Wells. There are many stylistic similarities between the eastern arm at Wells and features of the fabric, particularly some of the vaulting, of Exeter cathedral. Probably the whole of the eastern extension in Wells was conceived by Thomas of Witney, even though he did not complete it all. The Lady Chapel, for example, the first building of the new extension, is perfectly aligned on the old work, and the new work was clearly one scheme.

Witney certainly built all the chapels of the eastern arm and also most of the retroquire; a large imposing ambulatory built on such a scale to house the body of a possible saint (William of March, see Chapter 4). This attempt at canonization was abandoned by 1329 with the death of Bishop Drokensford, at about the same time that William Joy took over as master mason from Thomas of Witney. Evidence above the vaults of the retroquire shows the existence of fixings for flying buttresses, probably temporary, to support the eastern works before the extension of the quire was begun. These buttresses would have been built on the old east wall of the Lady Chapel of the original build. Because the vaulting of this whole space is evidently the work of two different people, it is possible to conclude that William Joy was working for Thomas of Whitney some while before he took over as master mason.

The elongated octagonal shape and what is in effect a domed roof was innovative in the extreme and showed Thomas of Witney's genius for design. He was also known for his great skill as a geometrician, particularly of spherical geometry. Linzee Colchester has given a simple explanation of the basic geometry used in the construction of the Lady Chapel: "Its plan can be simply fitted in between two equal overlapping circles, within a larger circle of which the radius equals the square root of twice the square of the radius of the small circles. And that large circle turned on edge produces an east-west section showing the vault, which is a perfect semi-circle in this plain [sic], with the circumference of its lowest point exactly touching the middle of the floor.".

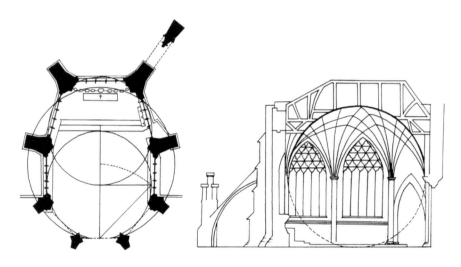

Left: Plan of the Lady Chapel, showing the basis of design (Colchester)
Right: A section through the Lady Chapel (Colchester)

Looking now at the striking features of the chapel itself, an upward gaze reveals all the intricacies of the star vault (opposite). The figure of Christ in Majesty showing his wounds is a symbol both of 'divine rulership and Judgement' (Ayers) and echoes back to the theme of the west front and the quire. Christ is the heart of the star from which the whole design radiates. The details of the main linking bosses have fine foliate designs, working from the centre, of vine, acanthus, oak and rose. Although the vault would certainly have been painted in medieval times, what can be seen now was created by Thomas Willement, the restorer of the east window in the mid nineteenth century. Apparently he offered to paint the vault free of charge

because of unbelievably prompt payment by the Dean and Chapter for his work on the window. He offered five designs to choose from of which the largest was selected. All the designs are preserved in the cathedral archives.

Because of the importance of the cult of the Virgin, the chapel was probably heavily painted throughout, including scenes depicted on the now bare walls.

There have been reports of shadows, shapes of figures and foliage and contours being seen, absorbed in the stone, bearing witness to this. The scenes would most likely have been below the string course, underneath a line of carved stone roses, a symbol of the Virgin, which themselves would also have been painted. However, the only real evidence of medieval paint to be detected is on the fifteenth century reredos, behind where the altar used to be. Evidence of bright red and gold are to be found in numerous places. This reredos, originally complete with statues was hideously mutilated in the seventeenth century. Puritan fanatics abhorred the cult of the Virgin as being the epitome of 'Popery'. In the twentieth century, Sir Charles Nicholson designed the wooden cresting at the top of the reredos, to finish off the stone in a tidy fashion, which had been brutally chopped off. The statue of the Virgin and Child (above) is by the sculptor A. G. Walker, created in the 1920s; later he made an almost identical statue for the Lady Chapel at Llandaff Cathedral.

Facing east, on the right are the sedilia (seats) for the mass and below them, a door. The sedilia date from the nineteenth century restoration; they do not appear in earlier prints or illustrations. The door leads into a medieval, tunnel-like passage which in turn would have led into a vestry or sacristy for the priests and also as an entrance during the period when the rest of the retroquire and the extension of the quire itself were being built. At this point the Lady Chapel may have been the only usable area for services.

There was generally a considerable amount of restoration and alteration in the nineteenth century, mainly because of the seventeenth century devastation both at the time of the Civil War and during Monmouth's rebellion of 1685. Earliest references date from 1642 and 1643, making it clear that not only Puritan soldiers but also civilians and even clergymen were involved in the destruction. Because it was a Lady Chapel, the devastation here was greater than elsewhere in the church and it was only from 1833 with the Oxford Movement that interest was revived in Our Lady.

The floor, originally of Doulting stone, was in such poor condition that a new 'Victorian' pavement was laid of Minton tiles. Part of this work was to create a top step leading to the altar which makes the reredos lower niches appear to sink into the ground. The tiles in the whole of this area are mainly factory produced but the more elaborate ones in blue are worth a look; they were designed by Pugin. In the very centre of the floor, directly under the figure of Christ in the vault, within the shape of a star are Christ the Lamb of God, surrounded by the symbols of the four evangelists (the winged man of St Matthew, the lion of St Mark, the ox of St Luke and the eagle of St John), so echoing the tracery tops of the glass in all five windows.

The Glass

The construction of the traceries, described by Colchester as 'a series of spherical triangles spiked' and by Ayers as 'fish-scale', has a profound impact on the appearance of all five windows. These are definitely the design of Thomas of Witney. The thickness of the base of each triangle is half that of the sides, which makes it much easier to see all the glass portrayed. Dating the glass in general is not easy as so many fragments come from other parts, mainly of the eastern arm of the cathedral, much of which is older than that of the Lady Chapel itself. Ayres describes the inserted glass in the main lights as coming predominantly from the chapter house, the north transept and the

The fragmented south-west window

retroquire chapels or quire aisles. What is certain is that in general, given a range of 1325-1330, the traceries were put in earlier than the main lights. It was often the case that larger windows were not glazed until the building was complete, although in this case it would be imperative to protect the canons from the elements when the chapel was used for services during the extension of the quire. What separates the traceries from the main lights in terms of dating is a complete absence of silver stain, whereas this does exist in the canopies of the main lights. The use of silver stain appeared somewhere between 1310 and 1320 when it was discovered that the application of a compound of silver on white glass produced a yellow tint when fired, which darkened if the quantity of silver compound was increased or the firing extended.

The Traceries

The traceries are worth a detailed look as most of the glass is original, even though patching has occurred over the centuries, whereas in the main lights only the canopies have generally survived. The symbols of the four evangelists flanking Christ (a nineteenth century addition) on either side in the tracery tops again echo the theme of the whole building. In the east window, Christ is shown attended by angels, presenting the instruments of the passion: the emblems of Christ's royalty and victory over death (Ayres). This then foreshadows the Second Coming. Facing east and reading from left to right are in the apex, the winged lion of St Mark (pictured), with the inscription S: MAR. CU. S. and underneath varying foliage of maple, ivy, vine and flower heads.

Continuing towards the east, the next tracery top shows the winged man of St Matthew (right) with the inscription S: MAT. HEVS. Underneath are nine of the sons of Jacob (there being no room for more) representing the patriarchs of the twelve tribes of Israel. On the right of the east window at the top is what remains of the eagle of St John, the lower wings and the talons. Underneath, to balance the patriarchs on the other side, are the

prelates and saints of the church, to demonstrate the New Law established by Christ. In both traceries flanking the east window there is one forward facing figure in the middle, the rest are facing inwards towards the centre, often made by a reverse image of the same cartoon. The final tracery top on the right should be the winged ox of St Luke of which no trace survives. Underneath are trefoils of foliage: oak, vine, ivy and acanthus and various flower heads.

The Main Lights

It is immediately apparent that the east window was restored in 1845 as already mentioned. Very little of the original scheme has survived except for the bottom panel, second from left, which shows the serpent complete with wings, wound round the Tree of the Knowledge of Good and Evil (right), offering the apple to Eve and part of an inscription: ARBOR CUM SERPERTE [sic]. The serpent's face was an addition by Willement. Willement himself described his task in a hand-written catalogue: "1845. The fine centre window…was taken down, cleaned, releaded and refixed. Several new figures of prophets etc. were added, where the old were imperfect". The restoration of this window has often been criticized for an over-dominant use of blue and red in the background of the figures but according to Ayers his choice of materials would have been limited "….For its period, his work was both thoughtful and respectful of the surviving remains". Apart from the serpent panel, all the figures are part of the restoration. Eve, on the far left is probably in the right place as the serpent in the next panel is inclining towards her. Mary is obviously a central figure

as the second Eve, where the first Eve led to The Fall, the second Eve is an instrument of Redemption. As a medieval figure she may have been placed higher up to give her greater prominence. This then leads to the Christ at the top and the Second Coming. Again the connection between the iconography of this window and the Jesse window and the west front is strong.

The other four windows are almost totally made up of fragments although the one immediately on the right of the east window, more obviously shows figures under the existing medieval canopies. This is the window very much worked on by Dean Armitage Robinson in the early 1920s. He also had a hand in the other "mosaic" windows, grouping together figurative subjects

and inscriptions, in order to be able to see them more clearly. By the autumn of 1924, releading of these four windows was underway. Much of the glass, as already mentioned, came from elsewhere. For example, in the middle main light of the most western left-hand window is a partial roundel depicting an angel with trumpet and beautifully textured wings (left), which originally belonged to the chapter house. In this same window are two shields, obviously not part of the original scheme. The lower is the shield of Mortimer of Richards Castle, seen as late as 1686 in the east aisle of the north transept, and above that the shield of Zouche, whose original position is unknown. Where borders still exist in all the windows there are the original designs of fleur de lys and lions. Some of the lions, on close inspection, are not in standard pose. One or two are looking over their shoulder, one is even scratching his nose: doing what lions do. Random fragments fill up the spaces. Any plain glass fragments of bright and pastel colours, used as fill in, probably are part of the consignment from France, bought by the cartload by Bishop Law (1824-45), most of which was used to decorate his palace.

Whatever the haphazard fragmentary appearance of most of these windows, the colours have never lost their vibrancy and to see them in their greatest glory is to be present at Morning Prayer on a sunny day, when a veritable prism of colour plays on the bare walls.

Modern Times

Given the importance of the Lady Chapel liturgically and historically and its frequent use today, it might appear to be rather spartan and bare. In 1999, the then Chancellor Melvyn Matthews conceived the idea of a re-ordering, of a return to a more contemplative space. All the old, dark nineteenth century furniture which cluttered it, including an 1860s organ, was removed. In addition the eastern focus of the altar was moved to the centre to emphasize the communality of worship, for it is here on most days that Morning Prayer at 7.30 a.m. is recited, as the start of the daily round of worship: the duty of cathedral canons since the church was built. The re-ordering has not to date been completed as it might entail major funding, and currently other priorities are manifold.

When still in existence, the Wells Theological College (1840-c.1972) used the Lady Chapel as its college chapel. Since then Morning Prayer, Eucharists, said Evening Prayer, and services such as the monthly healing service are held here, in addition to weddings, funerals, meditations, and recitals. It is also a space where many visitors come to sit, to think, to pray.

The Retroquire

Although the basic structure of the retroquire, connecting the new east end of the quire with the Lady Chapel has been discussed, it is worth noting the 'forest' of slim pillars which were improvised to marry the two structures safely. These again are identified with Thomas of Witney. Tierceron ribs emerge from the pillars, and where at the west end, by the east quire wall, there are a pair of ribs on each side which have nowhere to link to, the solution was to have lion heads swallowing them. Medieval masons liked tidy finishes, with nothing left drifting in mid air. Of the slim columns, the two at the west end each have a core of blue lias surrounded by shafts of Purbeck marble whereas the ones to the east are made from Purbeck marble throughout.

The large brass lectern (right) which dominates the centre of the retroquire (in the absence of any satisfactory saint), previously stood at the mouth of the Lady Chapel and before that, in the quire. It was given in 1661 by the dean, Robert Creyghtone as a thanksgiving for his position at Wells which was granted to him by the newly crowned king, Charles II. On either side of the lectern is an engraved explanation of Creyghtone's exile during the period of the Commonwealth, as chaplain to his king. The lectern was made to be placed sideways on to the congregation, with a large Old Testament on one side and the New Testament on the other. In this way the reader could be seen. The original Bible, also given by Creyghtone, was used until 1966 and is now held in the cathedral library. The lectern was made by William Burroughes, who also made lecterns for Canterbury and Lincoln and The Queen's College, Oxford. It has not been used for many years as it is rather impractical and extremely heavy to move.

Behind the lectern towards the west, on the back of the east wall of the quire are icons depicting the fourteen Stations of the Cross. These were painted in the year 2000 by Bulgarian artist Sylvia Demitrova, when she was artist-in-residence at the cathedral for a year. She studied in Bulgaria, first at Troyan, and further developed her skill in icon painting in Sofia, under the direction of the grand master, Georgi Tchouchev. Since marrying Simon Potter, then a housemaster at Downside School, she has made her life in England and her works can also be seen in the chapel of the Bishop's Palace and at Downside Abbey.

Further round at the north-east corner is some fine altar lace in a frame, made by Mrs C M Town between 1958 and 1966. She presented this to the cathedral in memory of her daughter who had died on active service in India in 1944.

Across from this corner, against the south side of the screen of St Stephen's Chapel, is a large ancient seal chest given to the cathedral by Bishop Ralph of Shrewsbury in the mid 1300s. This large, heavy chest, complete with five locks for safety, was made to prevent the chapter seal from being stolen or inadvertently lost; it was small enough to pocket, being about 7.5cm (3 inches) in diameter, making this a distinct possibility. Seal chests have a small ledge inside usually on the right to contain the seal and the rest of the considerable space would most likely have been used for valuable books and documents.

St Stephen's Chapel

Immediately behind the seal chest is the south facing screen of St Stephen's Chapel. The whole chapel with its altar, furnishings and screen was designed by Sir Ninian Comper, a well known architect and designer, in 1935. The Mothers' Union banner was also designed by him and it is here that the Mothers' Union hold their services. The remarkable screen (pictured opposite), which looks at first sight to have been made of metal, is in fact made of cleverly disguised wood. At the top are highly gilded and coloured scenes from the Nativity.

St Stephen's Chapel: Ninian Comper's screen

The Glass

The main lights of the east window are again made up of displaced medieval fragments, with only what remains of the canopies in place. In the lower panel of the middle light is a fragment of text (pictured below) referring to the cathedral's patron saint; 'Andrea ora pro nob(i)s', which is probably fifteenth century and, according to Ayers, may have originated on the Chain Gate. In the top tracery of the east window, is a well preserved censing angel swinging a censer in the right hand and holding a pale pink incense boat in the left. The wings are delicately outlined in white and murrey. The north window has Christ Enthroned in the top tracery, his right hand held up in blessing and his left holding an orb. On either side beneath him are two censing angels. This window balances the one on the other side in St John the Baptist's chapel, with similar heads of saints in the lower traceries. All the identifiable glass appears to be c.1330-1335.

Corpus Christi Chapel

This chapel is screened off by an elaborately carved wooden structure, the western part of which was found in the cow stalls of Lubborn House, Baltonsborough near Glastonbury. It was given to the cathedral by two sisters, the Misses Whitehead in 1927, in memory of their parents. The screen was extended to form a canopy over the tomb of Dean John de Godelee (1306-1333) which mirrors the tomb of his bishop, John Drokensford on the south side. It was bishop and dean together who drove on the building of the new eastern arm. Both effigies would originally have been covered with high and intricately carved canopies. This chapel with its half-drawn curtains is often used for private prayer.

Inside the chapel, to the left of the altar a candle burns under a curtained niche, which holds the reserved Sacrament (consecrated bread and wine representing the Body and Blood of Christ), always ready prepared for visits to the sick and the dying. To the right of the altar, is part of the trunk of an olive tree, cradling a flask of olive oil. Oil, used as far back as Biblical times as medicine and balm; as a means of anointing kings and bishops; in baptism and confirmation, brings soothing peace, gladness and joy.

Above the altar is a late medieval carving of the Ascension (left), which was previously in the east cloister. It was moved to its present position by George Kibble in 1866, and in 1975 the soft colouring of this sculpture was sympathetically restored by Maurice Keevil. On the north side by the altar is the tomb of Robert Creyghtone: he was successively treasurer, chaplain in exile to Charles II, created dean after the Restoration in 1660 and, as the ultimate reward, enthroned as bishop in the last two years of his life (1670-1672). His effigy, carved in alabaster, shows him in his episcopal finery, resting on a slab of Tournai marble. Below him in a recess under the north window, is reputed to lie John Middleton, who was chancellor of the cathedral for only three weeks in 1337, superseded by Simon de Bristol who had probably been promised the next vacant post. Middleton then became the bishop's commissary and lived on into the 1350s.

Roped off in the north-west corner are the only remaining medieval floor tiles still in situ; their fragility demands protection. Perhaps they were preserved because until 1976, the tomb of Bishop Gilbert Berkeley (1560-1581) covered most of them. Berkeley's tomb had been placed in the chapel to make way for the tomb of Bishop Kidder in the north transept in 1703 and moved to the north quire aisle in 1976, to leave more space for prayer in the chapel.

The Glass

The east window has very little medieval glass left in situ. In the main lights small panels made up of old glass from other parts of the cathedral, having been cleaned and re-arranged, were inserted. The work was carried out by Dennis King in 1984. The clearest figures are those in the right hand light, in the middle panel, where part of a crowned Virgin can be seen and inserted on the right is part of the figure of St Peter complete with the bottom part of his keys. The north window was completely re-created and inserted in 1902 by James Powell and Company. It was designed by G P Hutchinson and depicts the Virtues of Fortitude, Faith, Hope and Temperance. The west window has just a few fragments of medieval glass in the main light tops; parts of canopies (1330-1335), which were only placed in their present position in 1990.

The North Quire Aisle

Tomb of Bishop Giso of Lorraine (1060-1088)

Proceeding down the north quire aisle, on the south side is the tomb of Giso of Lorraine (1060-1088), the last of the Saxon bishops of the first cathedral. He was also the last to bear the title of Bishop of Wells. He expanded the old cathedral with monastic-type buildings for the canons; cloisters, refectory, dormitory, since the clergy had previously lived scattered about the town. He established a communal life based on the rule of St Chrodegang, eighth century bishop of Metz, whose rule was familiar to Giso and it could be applied particularly to secular (non-monastic) canons. He was also one of the few who survived in office after the Norman Conquest as he was known to favour William Duke of Normandy.

Tomb of Ralph of Shrewsbury (1329-1363)

Next is the tomb of Bishop Ralph during whose time most of the current presbytery was built. It was moved from its original place in the middle of the presbytery because it got in the way of the celebrants. The effigy is of alabaster, much marred by centuries old graffiti. It was Ralph who followed Bishop Drokensford and completed not only the eastern extension but

Tomb of Ralph of Shrewsbury, heavily graffitied

also Vicars' Hall and Close. He also crenellated his palace and had a moat dug, complete with gate-house, portcullis and drawbridge. It was during his episcopate that the scissor arches were built and then in 1348, when the Black Death menaced the community, he withdrew to his manor of Wiveliscombe and administered the diocese in comparative safety.

Ledger Stone of John Sellick
Inserted into the floor is the ledger stone of Dr John Sellick, Archdeacon of Bath, whose greatest claim to fame was to be sent, with a fellow clergyman and with the active support of Charles II, to negotiate the release of 162 sailors who had been captured and enslaved by the pirates of Algiers. The English clergy raised £10,000 in 1662 to buy their release. The other clergyman, Canon John Bargrave of Canterbury summed up the expedition: 'All the difficulties lay upon me by reason that my brother commissioner (Sellick) had never binn [sic] beyond the seas, nor could speak a word of their language, and so understood not his danger'. Although the mission was successful, subsequently the English consul Mr Brown was enslaved and eventually beaten to death.

The opening into the quire near the high altar rail was made by David Rice, the last master mason in the 1980s, who in true medieval tradition left his mark: a Z (the mark of Zorro) whose adventures he had avidly followed as a child. A small amount of whitewash can also be seen low down where the tomb of Ralph of Shrewsbury was moved to make way for the opening. This is a small patch of the 1550 lime wash vigorously applied to the cathedral by the Protestants. Opposite this, the new opening into the undercroft will be dealt with in the next chapter.

Tomb of Gilbert Berkeley (1560-1581)

This is the tomb removed from Corpus Christi chapel in 1976. Around the top of the tomb, there are two puzzles contained in the Latin texts. Several letters of the text round the edge were filled with orange wax (still faintly visible) and if these are treated as Roman numerals, they give the year of his death. The inscription in the middle will give his age if the first word of the first two lines, again are treated as Roman numerals, namely VI XI and L V XI, adding up to eighty-three.

Further west are the last two Saxon bishops in the series of seven.

The Sacristy

On the north side before the corner where the aisle meets the north transept, is a door marked 'Private', which leads to the sacristy where communion vestments and vessels are kept. This is not open to the public but was originally the only entrance to the undercroft from the interior of the cathedral. It is in effect a wide passage way which ends in a massive door, now kept permanently shut. Inside this space, there are some large roof bosses, for once almost at head height as the vaulted ceiling is low. The detail of some of the bosses is remarkable. There is a large head of a green man just inside the door, and further along are two green men joined at the head. Other subjects include a donkey and a ram; others are difficult to interpret as many bits are missing.

The Glass

Looking from the east at the first window, there is medieval glass in the traceries with at the top, the figure of St Michael; the same cartoon has been used as on the south side opposite, but in reverse. This one is better preserved and shows St Michael spearing a fierce-looking dragon with his left hand. One bare foot seems to be standing on the dragon's tail, with the other pinning down his wing. All the tracery lights have glass dated 1330-1335. In the main lights three shields have been inserted, on the left that of Thomas Duke of Clarence (d.1421) brother of Henry V, framed with much earlier fragmented glass; the shield of Mortimer: The Royal Arms of England. All three shields have been dated by Ayers as early fifteenth century.

The second window moving towards the west, has the Crucifixion in the top tracery, and although the figure is incomplete, clearly visible are his feet, separately nailed to the cross. Underneath are the figures of the Virgin (to the left) and St John (to the right). This glass is again dated 1330-1335 although Colchester thinks this may have been earlier because of the separated feet. In the main lights are three shields, on the left the shield of Clerk (Bishop John Clerk 1523-1541): the shield of Wells, bearing the saltire cross of St Andrew: the shield of William Knight (bishop 1541-1547). All are dated between 1537 and 1547. According to Colchester these shields were probably inserted by William Knight himself.

The third window shows St John the Baptist (left) in the top tracery with a fine if tortured face, holding the Agnus Dei in his right hand and pointing to it with his left; this and all the other glass in the traceries is dated 1330-1335. In the main lights are again three shields, the first is probably of Richard Woleman (dean 1529-1537): the Royal Arms of England with only the fleur de lys clearly showing; it is surrounded by a garter of blue glass with the familiar motto 'HONY SOIT QVI NAL Y PENCE' [sic]: the third shield again is bishop William Knight who probably inserted all three shields. All the shields are dated 1537-1547.

The fourth window is entirely different as it was created and inserted in 1885 through the efforts of Dean Plumptre, to celebrate the bicentenary of Thomas Ken's consecration as Bishop of Bath and Wells (1685-1691).Bishop Ken appears to have been one of the most saintly of bishops, much admired to the present day for his integrity. The window (below) is entirely painted in enamels; it is full of figures and texts and is very difficult to read, as it is over-cluttered. Central in the centre light is Bishop Ken in full pontificals and underneath him are his Arms impaled with those of the See. The window was created by Philip Westlake and completed after his death by his brother, N. H. J. Westlake, both of the firm of Westlake and Barraud. To read this window in detail, binoculars are recommended.

The Chapter House from the vestibule

Chapter 7
The Chapter House and its Undercroft

Entering the undercroft through the archway and door on the north side of the north quire aisle, it is hardly noticeable that this entrance was newly created in 2008 to provide visitor access, so skilfully has the medieval wall (part 12th and part 14th century) been breached. This work was carried out by the Clerk of the Works and his team and behind the door on the right and also by the smaller door which leads directly into the undercroft, are two modern mason's marks of a fleur de lys, belonging to Mark Rowe, the mason on the team. It was he and Michael Haycraft (the Clerk of the Works) who were mainly responsible for the work on this section. The archway is beautifully finished off, as are the breached medieval wall benches. In addition Michael Haycraft made the door using medieval-type methods and fixings. The result is an object of beauty and admiration.

Construction
Usually a chapter house is situated on the south side attached to a cloister but this at Wells proved impossible once it had been decided to keep the old Lady Chapel-by-the-Cloister, part of the first cathedral. Indeed this lady chapel was used as a chapter house from time to time before the current one was complete. Both the undercroft and chapter house are octagonal in shape, which at this period was quite fashionable. The idea of a polygonal shape for chapter houses dates from the early twelfth century (Rodwell). For example at Worcester in the early twelfth century there was a circular chapter house with ten flat-buttressed segments, which was the precursor of the Wells octagon and among others the designs of Salisbury, Lincoln and Westminster Abbey.

Stone mason Mark Rowe, working on the new undercroft doorway in 2008

The dating of the undercroft, which served as a crypt and a treasury, is tentative as it was definitely built in two phases; lack of money and manpower probably hindering a continuous construction. Visible round the walls are two different types of tooling (the finishing off of the stone blocks). For approximately two metres (6 ft+) from ground level the tooling is diagonal and further up, horizontal. The first part of the construction was probably made early in the 1200s, including the laying out of the whole outline. Jerry Sampson says that the stoppage may have occurred to enable the masons to concentrate on the completion of the west front and that in the period immediately following, money had run out, partly due to expensive litigation in Rome concerning Bishop Jocelin's successor.

It is known that work had begun again by 1286 when the walls and vault were completed and the steps to the chapter house under construction. This renewed campaign ended in 1306 when the chapter house was complete. Above the chapter house is a wooden roof to support the lead, the vault having been made of tufa, a lightweight porous limestone found reasonably locally. This tufa stone only occurs in the roof of the Lady Chapel, the retroquire and the chapter house. In the same way the timber construction is similar in all three, in that they are all integrated with the masonry, since either they receive support from the tufa vault or they are strutted off it. Harvey draws the conclusion that all three must have been the work of the same master carpenter. In the chapter house complex, each level of construction, one above the other, has a central pillar. In the undercroft it is like an immensely thick stumpy tree made of stone, and above that, in the chapter house, is an elegant shafted central pillar with thirty-two ribs emerging from it as part of the tierceron vault: like a palm tree touching the sky (pictured below). The final "tree" is of wood as it forms part of the structure holding up the lead; it looks like the enormously fat trunk of an ancient oak.

The Undercroft

The passageway which now links the north quire aisle to the undercroft stands on what was once open, if rather soggy ground which had an unused lean-to on the left and a large boiler house on the right: now on the left is the Ken Biggs Room (after the builder of the development project) used as a greenroom for visiting choirs and orchestras with space and storage also for embroiderers and flower arrangers; on the right is a substantial storage room. The bases of the immense stepped buttresses which are visible in the passageway were of course originally external, and discovered to be underpinned when the latest building works in this area were underway. It is known that when the undercroft was constructed, much levelling of ground, to correct a north-south slope, was carried out and over time some of those materials had been washed away thus destabilizing the foundations. The underpinning was first carried out in

1898 when there is a record of an order for 17,000 blue Staffordshire bricks, 24 tons of cement, 20 tons of sand and 34 loads of aggregate. The total cost came to £210 and was paid for personally by Chancellor Bernard as the Dean and Chapter were short of money.

Entering the undercroft itself, the archway of the small open door has been raised by about 30 cm (1 ft) to provide enough headroom for present day regulations. The new additional stone is self-evident from the inside. To the left of the door is the beginning of the interpretation display, putting the cathedral into the context of its background in terms of place, geology, water and building stone; many of the people who contributed and now contribute to the life and evolution of this great building; artefacts of interest through the ages and above all a sense of history which incorporates the spiritual life of the community.

Close to the beginning are two doors (left) which were the only access in medieval times to the undercroft since it was constructed to be a treasury, literally for the cathedral's treasures and also valuable manuscripts. Both doors were subjected to dendrochronology (tree-felling date) at the same time as the cope chest, by the Oxford Dendrochronology Laboratory. The inner door has a tree-felling date of c.1265. This is contemporary with the second phase of the undercroft building and is made in similar fashion to the great doors at the west end of the cathedral. It is hinged to open inwards and consists of vertical planks strengthened by a 'portcullis' frame. The iron scroll work which decorates it, with clusters of leaves, flowers and small birds, does not readily fit the wood and may have been recycled; the work is comparable to that at Windsor which is dated c.1249. In addition, above the door is a 'bolt hole' where a huge bar could be dropped down over the closed door at night; real belt and braces for the greatest security. The outer door is a couple of centuries later, fitted at the time of Bishop Bekynton when there were issues of security making it necessary to safeguard money, plate and jewels; there are several references in the communar's accounts for 1449-1450 to expenses on account of "the insurgents against the peace of the church and the king". The tree-felling date is c.1450. It is a massive door with an impressive lock and bolting system, strengthened by the method of construction; vertical planks on one side and horizontal planks on the other. This door is kept permanently closed as the sacristy is on the other side of it.

Taking a circular tour of the display cases, in the middle near the entrance/exit door, there is an enormous stone coffin which was found beneath the east cloister in the 1700s. It is the coffin of a priest of some importance, as it contains a niche to hold the chalice and paten. It dates from the thirteenth century when the first east cloister was built. Also of note before leaving, on the left of the small door is a medieval lavabo with an unusual carving of a dog lying flat, gnawing on a bone (below).

One last glance round this calm and rugged space makes it almost impossible to imagine how much this area was disrespected in the previous two centuries. In the nineteenth it was used as a coke hole to service the huge boilers of that era and then in the twentieth century it was the depository of all kinds of furniture, staging and a certain amount of junk which no one seemed to know what to do with. In addition, part of it was a chorister practice room complete with piano and another part acted as vestry for the choristers (latterly boys and girls) and the vicars choral; sometimes it was like negotiating an obstacle course. For practical reasons alone it is no wonder that a purpose built song-school was required.

The Steps

Entrance to the steps which lead to the chapter house is by way of the door at the north end of the east aisle of the north transept. This door appears very much squeezed to the left of the tomb of Thomas Cornish because of the chapel which once stood there. According to Warwick Rodwell the intention would have been to create 'a great doorway centred on the newly built stair', for processions to pass easily up to the chapter house; this never happened.

The steps were not as they are seen today as mounting towards the north, where there is now an archway with steps leading to the Chain Bridge and thence to Vicars' Hall. There was originally just a window identical to those on the west side of the staircase and the steps curved round to the right into the chapter house itself. These steps are among the most photographed and filmed of any area in the cathedral, with the wear of generations of trudging feet clearly visible in the stone. Some steps have had to be replaced for reasons of safety as they had become too worn and slippery; before that the steps looked like a great wavy sea of stone disappearing romantically towards the north. There are some old photographs which show this.

As already mentioned, rooflines of the temporary vestry are clearly visible at the bottom of the steps and just beyond are two corbels, one on either side, of two clerics each rather casually killing a dragon by thrusting a stick down the gullet with their left hands and the one on the right in equally nonchalant manner, is supporting the entire building with his right hand. Under the windows on the left are small steps, between the modern banister and the wall, which were in fact seats for witnesses giving evidence when the Dean and Chapter presided over legal matters. On the east wall high up is a barred window-opening which brings some light to what was probably a store room, accessed by the separate staircase which leads to the chapter house roof. It is one of these incidental spaces, in this case between the staircase and the chapter house vestibule, which could prove useful; several such spaces or rooms are found in various parts of the cathedral.

On the west side in the large windows lighting the steps, is the oldest glass in the cathedral, still present in all the top traceries except one. This glass dates from c.1290 and according to Tim Ayers all the glass in the main lights was probably similar to that in the parish church of Acton Burnell, at the time when Bishop Burnell (1275-1292) built the new hall and church in Acton Burnell, the chapel and the great hall in the Bishop's Palace at Wells and much of the chapter house steps. Probably the main lights were of grisaille, as is the white glass still evident in the traceries, to let in as much light as possible. The foliage in the grisaille glass is an early example, in English stained glass, of a naturalistic approach. The one much cleaner top tracery is a copy of the original which was cleaned by the conservation department of the Victoria and Albert Museum in London in 1967/68; the original is in store as after a very careful cleaning process it was considered to be too fragile to be exposed to the weather. All the other tracery lights suffer from a heavy lime deposit showing darkly and reducing their translucency. There is evidence that all this remaining glass has been repaired and re-ordered many times.

Two smaller pieces of glass worth noting, both from the fifteenth century, are further up the staircase which leads to the Chain Bridge. On the right in the tracery nearest the top of the steps is a most delicate representation of St Barbara (right). She is haloed and has long tresses of hair hanging down her back. There is much use of silver stain particularly noticeable in the tower which she holds in her right hand and also what is probably the host in her left. The glass was cracked but has fairly recently been repaired and restored. Tim Ayers gives the date as c.1460. There is a slightly earlier roundel (1320-1340) on the left where the steps lead onto a flat surface close to the door; it was originally part of the scheme of the Vicars' Chapel at the end of Vicars' Close and depicts the arms of the See. It had found its way into private hands but was returned to the cathedral by the owner, on condition that it could be seen and enjoyed by visitors. As there was anyway no room in the glass of the chapel which had been re-ordered in the nineteenth century, it is now as close to the Vicars' complex as possible yet visible to all.

The Chapter House
The Vestibule

There is no access for visitors to the chain bridge and beyond, so it is necessary to follow the stairs which veer off to the right, so encountering, first, the vestibule. Although perhaps not immediately apparent, the vestibule is constructed in the shape of a rhomboid and not a rectangle. This is more obvious looking from the inside outwards, as the cusped heads of the arches of the stone doorways with their cusped spherical triangles above are not in line, giving, according to Colchester, an impression of an interwoven crown of thorns. This shape may have been because during the gap between the commencement of the chapter house complex and its re-starting in c.1286, design of windows had altered and the decorated style had come in, thus making bay sizes larger. This meant that the present second bay was no longer exactly opposite the centre of the west wall of the octagon.

The coloured stone, used by way of contrast, with some very fine leaf carving on the capitals, comes from an unusual bed of blue lias which has larger fossils embedded in it. This has sometimes caused it to be described as purbeck marble although typically the fossilized shells in that stone are much smaller. Indeed the only purbeck marble found in this whole area is one inward facing shaft of the central pillar nearest the chapter house itself and all the contrasting stone of the central column of the interior, including the seat.

It was in the vestibule that an official sat to guard the privacy of the chapter

house. According to Colchester, wooden doors closed off the chapter house although there is now no sign of any fixings. It is also possible that screens of some sort might have been used. Above in the vaulting is an interesting central boss (right) which on first glance could consist of curly leaves, a common motif. However, on closer inspection there are four identical heads of an old, bearded man, with all four beards meeting at the centre and the top of the heads facing outwards. The 'doorkeeper' might have to sit for hours keeping watch, especially on days when the Chapter was in session as an ecclesiastical court, with witnesses sitting on the seats by the steps. On the stone bench on the left hand side of the vestibule is an inserted stone with a board game scratched on it; this may have been placed there as a diversion for hours of tedious waiting.

The Interior

Many visitors audibly gasp on entering the chapter house. Its beauty, its lightness and the feeling of soaring upwards, enhanced by the slender central column, is overwhelming, particularly when sunshine streams through the windows. This is a truly 'decorated' space with detailed stone sculpture adding to the play of light and shade. All the window embrasures are decorated with ballflower, probably the earliest example of this design, as elsewhere there is no record before 1307. The central column with its sixteen purbeck shafts captures the eye immediately and directs the gaze upwards to the thirty two spreading ribs, like a great palm tree touching the sky. These ribs of a tierceron vault, fan out to join the ridge ribs at an angle linked by beautifully carved bosses of oak, vine and ivy, at least one green man and a lady with long tresses linking to the foliage which surrounds her: she is not easy to see. Tierceron vaulting was much in use in the decorated period; it is defined by ribs rising directly from the tops of the pillar shafts, also to be seen in the retroquire. Having remarked on the lightness of this space it should also be noted that this would not have been the case in medieval times. A glance round the canopies and head stops of the stalls reveals evidence of red paint and of course all the windows would have contained coloured glass, thereby darkening the interior considerably.

Round the outer walls on seven sides of the octagon (the eighth is open to the vestibule) are forty-nine stalls for prebendaries or canons, with an extra fiftieth one near the open archway, left by tradition for St Andrew (patron saint), should he be inclined to drop in on the proceedings. Each stall has a canopy supported by blue lias shafts and above head height are brass plates giving the name of each prebend. A prebend was an estate, village or community from which the prebendaries or canons drew their income. Most prebends were quite small with only one prebendary attending chapter meetings but the large manor of 'Comba' (several manors collectively), now called Combe St Nicholas, divided its revenues among fifteen prebendaries; Wedmore, a village not far from Wells, had five. The brass plates were put up in 1883.

Each stall is decorated by head stops (pictured opposite), roughly divided into popes on the east side, lawyers on the west and bishops and kings between the two. All the corner head stops, two at each, are comical in some way; two are sticking out their tongues, some have inane grimaces. There are one or two missing at the corners, which Colchester suggests may have been hacked off as being too disreputable. All head stops are identified by their head gear such as crowns and mitres, lawyers are evident by their coifs which they wore to keep fleas out of their ears, rife in public places. These

coifs were replaced in Charles II's time with wigs. The prebendaries sat on the upper seats and their vicars, when present, on the lower ones; choristers had to stand. The dignitaries (that is the dean, chancellor, precentor, treasurer, and archdeacon of Wells) sat at the east end with a stall in the middle of this row for the bishop. This has hardly been occupied since Bishop Drokensford was denied access in 1319. From that moment the bishop, who still had the right of Visitation, could only occupy his seat with the consent of the Dean and Chapter, which was seldom granted. Even today, the bishop does not set foot in the chapter house on official occasions, so strong is tradition. Over the top of the bishop's stall are the repainted arms of James I, showing the Order of the Garter.

The whole chapter house, which measures 16.1 metres (53 feet 6 inches) across, was comprehensively cleaned in 1989-1990; all the blue lias shafts were rubbed down and a coat of polish was applied, masons' marks around the walls became more visible with the grime and dust removed and the glass was cleaned and re-glazed. Not so easy to identify are a series of marks on the floor towards the east side which, according to Warwick Rodwell were originally identified by Irvine as the layout for a fan vault, possibly that above the central tower or of Stillington's chapel (now no longer there); both would have been designed by master mason William

Smyth. The marks are now very faint as hundreds of feet pass over them year by year and Doulting stone is notorious for wear.

The Glass

The price paid for the present lightness of the interior is that very little remains of the original medieval glass, some of the earliest in the building. It only now survives in the traceries as most was destroyed during the Civil War and the period of the Commonwealth. Some fragments of chapter house

glass are to be found in other parts of the building. Mention has already been made of the angel with trumpet, now in the Lady Chapel but originally in one of the large roundels at the top of the tracery. The smaller roundels which still survive contain a depiction in each of two of the dead rising from their tombs on the Day of Judgement (left), again echoing the west front theme. In the non-figurative tracery lights, in the pointed trefoils, there is white foliage against a ruby background. Most are of vine but there are some representations of maple, possibly echoing the bosses of the vault. In all the non-figurative glass, since the cleaning process in 1989-1990, the ruby colour has a vivid and vibrant quality.

Use

Nowadays the chapter house is used only for ceremonial purposes; chapter meetings are held in the chapter room in the office complex below the Vicars' Hall. This is no different from the average company board room with a large table down the centre; far more practical for conducting the business of the cathedral, since the chapter house, apart from lacking various facilities, is very cold in winter. The modern Chapter in Wells is composed of the five clerical dignitaries (known in medieval times as the 'quinque') and three or four lay canons who are called prebendaries to differentiate them from their priestly colleagues. There are also about thirty prebendaries from the diocese; an honorary title in recognition of loyal and conspicuous service. These form part of the College of Canons which meets with the Chapter once a year. Ceremonial use of the chapter house is confined to the installation of new canons and prebendaries, following the main installation in Quire. This short ceremony is still conducted in Latin (various pronunciations can be heard around the chamber) and the bishop, although very much present in the installation ceremony in quire, is left at ground level while the Chapter and the new canon or prebendary ascend the steps to the chapter house. Apart from this specific ceremony, the chapter house is used for art exhibitions from time to time and offers a good space for school workshops: dance, story telling and drama.

This is all a far cry from the Middle Ages, when the chapter house was a symbol of the corporate authority and pre-eminence of the Chapter, even in secular cathedrals such as Wells. When the chapter house was completed in 1306 it illustrated the climax of the Chapter's ascent to power, followed a little later during the time of Bishop Drokensford (1319) by the ending of the episcopal hold over the cathedral. Starting with Bishop Jocelin, statutes were issued to define and codify existing practice for the clergy and adapt them to contemporary needs (Harvey).

Around 1300, Wells took over the Use of Sarum, a form of prescribed liturgy developed at Salisbury. As in many other secular cathedrals, Wells altered the Sarum Use to fit its own building and customs. The Wells version known as the Consuetudinary (what was customary practice day by day) is very specific about participation in Chapter meetings. Every day after Prime at around 9.30 in the morning, the assembled clergy, vicars choral and choristers processed to the chapter house for a morning meeting, where one of the vicars read the lesson. Part of the Martyrology (list of saints) was recited in relation to any saint who was to be commemorated on a particular day, obits (for the dead) were delivered and any domestic notices given out, such as, on Saturdays, the complete roster for the services and ministers for the following week. This part was the responsibility of the Precentor. Here also any rebukes concerning inappropriate behaviour were delivered by the dean or whichever member of the 'quinque' was presiding; fines could be imposed at this stage. Gradually over time this formal attendance of all the cathedral community in quire lessened.

In addition, meetings in the chapter house might be focussed on matters of the estate, of which the Chapter owned a considerable amount; there were also debates over finances. When the Chapter sat in its legal capacity it dealt with disputes over rents or tithes and misdemeanours of vicars choral or clergy which were not unknown. In such cases, witnesses could be summoned from the seats by the steps. After testimony had been given, witnesses had to sit on the seat round the central pillar until the process had ended; an uncomfortable position with all eyes from all sides upon them. It could be said that with such intimidation, the opinion of the Dean and Chapter always held sway!

The Library looking south towards the Muniment Room

Chapter 8
Cloisters and Environs

The Library

Before entering the east cloister by way of the tall south transept door, note a much smaller door immediately to the left. This gives access to a short spiral staircase which leads up to the library; built in the first half of the fifteenth century it occupies the whole length of the upper storey above the east cloister. This was the first of the early thirteenth century cloisters to be re-built under Bishop Bubwith, work commencing in c.1420, four years before his death. How far both the cloister and the library above had progressed is not known but Bishop Bubwith left sufficient funds in his will for its completion.

The library was most probably built in two stages starting from the northern end as far as eight bays. Recent dendrochronology on the library roof timbers gives a tree-felling date of c.1450 and the east cloister itself was finally paved with Doulting stone in 1457 when the library must have been ready for business.

Layout

The stairs lead to what is now the reading room where scholars of all descriptions can come and work and use the books in situ. This part is also open to visitors on most days although a rule of quiet applies if there are readers working. Looking towards the south, the iron-railed gate leads to the old chained library and visitors can catch a glimpse of what is there. Beyond the chained library, at the far south end, through solid wooden doors is the muniment room, where older archives are kept. Visitors can only enter the old library and the muniment room if a group tour is booked through the cathedral office. The original old library was smaller than at present and ended where the panelled wall narrows. Its length was increased in the early seventeen hundreds to house more books. Originally the present reading room and the north end of the old library were used as a long gallery; a place where the canons walked, thought and talked.

The Muniment Room

All the ancient documents and some highly valued books are kept here. Considering that during the seventeenth century most of the library's original books were lost, it is remarkable that so many documents and records survived. The records of the Dean and Chapter contain over 900 original deeds dating from 958 onwards. There are four cartularies or registers; the

A selection of documents from across several centuries

Liber Albus 1, Liber Ruber, Liber Albus II and Liber Fuscus, all defined by the colour of their covers. This series began c.1240 but contains copies of much older deeds, ranging from the time of Edward the Confessor to c.1500. From 1571 there is a continuous series of Chapter Acts books; more modern record books begin in 1837 and continue into the twentieth century. The greater part of the records relate to the administration of the Dean and Chapter estates until they were taken over by the Ecclesiastical Commissioners in the 1860s. Also kept here are the Vicars Choral records from 1348 when they were formed into a college. In addition there are records of the Wells Old Almshouses with deeds dating back to the thirteenth century.

Apart from documents there are certain prized manuscript books, mostly acquired through gifts since the original collection was destroyed or had decayed. Among the most special are: a fragment of the Benedictine Rule dating from the tenth or eleventh century both in Latin and Anglo-Saxon; a mid thirteenth century copy of Isidore of Seville's Liber Ethimologiarum and a thirteenth century Vulgate. The beautifully written and decorated Psalter of 1514 from Hailes Abbey is preserved here as well as a Latin translation of the Homilies of St Chrysostom dated 1517.

One special artefact which has found its way into the muniment room and now stands in the seventeenth century fireplace, is a late sixteenth century brass cauldron (right) which originally hung in the fireplace of the medieval kitchen in Vicars' Hall. It has recently been dated by Roderick and Valentine Butler and is a rare survival of its period. It was removed from the medieval kitchen for safe-keeping, since that is now used for the commercial operation of the cathedral catering company.

The Chained Library

The chained library as it is today has no surviving furniture from medieval times. The presses (bookcases) furthest to the south, five in all, date from 1685/86 and are made of pine. Much destruction had occurred during the period of the Commonwealth and after the Restoration of Charles II in 1660 the funds of the cathedral and its canons first went to the restoration and upkeep of the main body of the church. Not till March 1670 was any money set aside for the repair of the library. At the time of Monmouth's Rebellion in 1685 the library was ready to be refurnished and although the rebellion held up proceedings by virtue of some of the rebel soldiers being held in the cloister underneath, all the new presses were in place by the end of 1686. During the Commonwealth the books had been sent to the parish church of St Cuthbert with the idea of creating a lending library for the citizens of Wells. Although it is not known how many books actually were sent there, only around 200 books were ever returned and from the time of re-opening, the library was dependent on gifts and the legacies of the libraries of bishops and canons. In 1672, Dr Richard Busby, Headmaster of Westminster School and also Treasurer of the cathedral and a noted bibliophile, gave a substantial financial contribution and also a number of books to the library which certainly galvanized efforts to produce a functioning library again.

The new double-sided presses were very wide and at right angles to the windows to ensure that light fell on each sloping desk; this meant that alternate windows were blocked in, where the carefully positioned two sides of the presses met. The blocked windows can be seen clearly from the cloister garth below. A number of presses were needed because printed books were becoming more plentiful. The books in the chained library are by no means all concerned with theology but reflect the various interests of the donors: subjects as varied as law, history, science, medicine, poetry, travel and exploration and languages. By the late seventeenth century most of the books were not chained except for the most important ones and the last recorded purchase of chains was in 1734-35. Around this time (1728), three more presses were added, noticeable by their slightly lighter pine, to accommodate a large gift of books from Bishop George Hooper (1703-1727), a great scholar and linguist. There is one half press at the northern end which is part of the older furniture. It is covered by a wooden grille and was used to protect small books and possibly some documents.

Among the books donated over time are some treasures. For example, the earliest printed book in the library is Pliny's 'Natural History', printed in Venice in 1472, five years before the first book was printed in England. Also printed in Venice between 1495 and 1498, are five volumes of 'Aristotle and Theophrastus', once owned by Erasmus who wrote his signature in both Greek and Latin at the beginning and end of each volume. These books were given to the library by Dean William Turner, himself a scholar and author, of the 'New Herbal', the first book of its kind in English, published in 1568. This can also be found on the shelves.

William Turner's 'New Herbal'

This part of the library also houses the Vicars Choral library which was much battered and neglected after the College of Vicars was abolished. The books had been stored for a while on the Chain Bridge where damp was rife. Their library was originally in a room above the chapel in Vicars' Close, used subsequently by the Cathedral School. In the same way the Bath Abbey Collection had been neglected and was brought here to be looked after in 1982. When the floor of the old library was examined in 1999 it was discovered that the exceptionally wide boards visible in places, were in fact re-cycled ends of the original fifteenth century reading desks, used when re-flooring took place after the Restoration.

The Reading Room

There is one rare example of a fifteenth century reading desk in this part of the library (right). It is badly damaged and badly patched and the legs have been shortened. The sloping top would have held chained books lying flat and inside the cupboards underneath would have been more books lying flat and also chained. The doors are interesting in that they are very similar to those of the

lockers in the Vicars' treasury and also in the furniture of the small counting house or office inside the north wall of the north transept. These all date satisfactorily to the middle of the fifteenth century.

After this part of the library ceased to be a long gallery, it still had its original floor of beaten earth, even when Canon C. M. Church furnished the area in 1885 to house the accumulated nineteenth century books. These more modern presses, both double sided, were moved to the west cloister in 1972 so that the space could be used as an exhibition area in the summer season, based on the collections in the chained library and in the archives, usually on a given theme.

In the year 2000 a development began, spearheaded by the then chancellor Canon Melvyn Matthews to create a modern reading room with a new oak floor and new furniture built by local craftsmen. The nineteenth century presses

were also returned to this area and now house all the more modern books from 1800 onwards. It is a tranquil place for study and a wonderful setting which successfully manages to combine things both ancient and modern.

The roof is original all the way through and is supported by sixteen corbels, twelve of which are medieval. The medieval corbels are re-cycled and supported a possible upper storey of the original thirteen century cloister (Rodwell). Some of the heads which in most cases are topped by abaci and in one or two cases, stiff leaf foliage (old library), still contain traces of polychromy including pink, deep red, ochre and green. Along the east wall in both parts of the library, medieval stained glass can be seen, in particular the arms of Bishop Bubwith (three holly wreaths), the royal arms of England and, in one case, the arms of the see. Round the walls are prints and photographs of various parts and stages of the cathedral's life and one or two artefacts: a late thirteenth century cast-lead crucifix probably belonging to the tomb of Bishop Burnell (1275-1292), and the delicate head of a crozier, probably belonging to Bishop Jocelin

(1206-1242), made of copper gilt with inlaid Limoges enamel (it dates from the time when Bishop Jocelin might well have been in Limoges during the period of his exile). His Episcopal ring is in the same case. A modern facsimile of the exquisitely illuminated Lindisfarne Gospels of c.700, can

be seen in a centrally positioned display case. The most recent artefact on show, to the left of Jocelin's crozier is a small wooden pillar with three shafts and a certain amount of early medieval paint (pictured left); on the back is a Roman number IX. It may have belonged to a retable; a decorated wooden panel behind an altar, containing architectural features such as niches and arcades. It dates between the end of the thirteenth or beginning of the fourteenth century. In the visitor season there are two cases displaying books from the old library and some archives, to illustrate an event such as a notable anniversary which helps to give visitors a taste of what the library holds.

The library has always been and still is the private library of the Chapter. It contains about 6000 books which have been added to in recent years through a very modest budget. Until the mid twentieth century the library received an annual grant of £10 from the common fund of the cathedral. Nowadays it is funded by the Chapter and has a part time archivist and a part time librarian; both will take booked groups on tours of the chained library and the muniment room. This can be arranged via the cathedral office.

A more detailed account of the library and its contents can be found in an excellent booklet on sale both in the library and in the cathedral shop.

The Cloisters

Construction

Very little is left of the thirteenth century cloister of Bishop Jocelin's time (commencing c.1196), apart from the outer walls which were retained during the fifteenth century re-construction on all three sides. Modern scholars agree that in the original plan a north cloister walk was also envisaged; had this been completed and retained the four cloisters would have formed a perfect square with an outer dimension of c.51 metres (135 ft). There is some evidence that a north walk was built at least in part (Rodwell) but may have been abandoned fairly early on. According to Sampson there was no need processionally for a north walk at all, since there were impressive processional doors leading into the cathedral from the east and the west walks. It would in any case have left an awkward gap between the north walk and the south wall of the nave, although there is the example in Salisbury of this space being used for a plumbery (the workshop where plumbers worked the lead).

Another on-going discussion is whether the east cloister of the late twelfth and early thirteenth century was narrower than the other two when first built. This idea is largely based on the off-centre position of the door at the south end (the bishop's door), which leads towards the palace and was his private entrance into the cathedral; this is still the case today. There is no other physical evidence and it is possible that this was just a misjudged construction. Looking the other way from south to north, both in the east and the west cloister the tall doors into the cathedral are also not centralized and look uncomfortably squeezed. From the cathedral side however these doors stand centrally in a bay or aisle and as the cloisters were not completed until the west front was well underway, this off-centre effect from the cloister side may just be a miscalculated abutment. Whatever the case of a narrower east cloister possibility (Rodwell), there is little doubt that still within the thirteenth century the cloister was constructed to be the same width as that of the south and west. There is evidence of a thirteenth century capital and abacus on the left of the door into the south transept at the present width. It is also now fairly certain that this early cloister already contained a upper storey as at present, with a staircase to it in roughly the same place as the present fifteenth century octagonal stair turret. The roofs of all three thirteenth century cloisters were single slopes or pentices, the slope leaning inwards into the cloister garth. There is evidence of this inside the present roof structure, of roof lines and lead chases.

The present cloisters are part of a slow, piecemeal reconstruction of the fifteenth century, with a starting date for the east cloister of c.1420-1455

The East Cloister by night

(Bubwith, 1407-1424); followed by the west cloister in the mid 1400s until c.1480 (largely Bekynton) and a completion date for the south cloister of 1508 (Bishops Stillington to King).

East Cloister

As already mentioned, Bishop Bubwith began the major reconstruction of the east cloister and the library above but died long before the work was completed in the 1450s. He may have built as far as eight bays where the thickness of the buttresses alters. This is the only cloister where there is no

remaining evidence of the inner thirteenth century wall, the reconstruction being more comprehensive from the ground upwards than in the other two. The present inner wall with its perpendicular tracery is continued throughout the cloisters. It was originally only glazed above the transom (stone cross-bar). The tracery design can be seen in part on the medieval tracing floor, in the triforium above the north porch (Arnold Pacey).

East cloister tracery

A curiosity of this cloister is that the first bay from the south transept is not full width and although built first, the planning was from the south-east corner by the bishop's door; the spacing did not quite work. On the right looking down the cloister is the main entry into the cloister garth and on the left just south of this is a break in the thirteenth century wall bench. Here was the entrance to the Chapel of the Holy Cross, the base of whose outer walls can be seen from the Camery. South of the gap is the entrance to the Camery itself: the arched doorway built to enter Bishop Stillington's impressive Lady Chapel in the late fifteenth century. Just down from this is the blocked arched doorway of the original Lady Chapel-by-the-Cloister which was preserved when the thirteenth century cloister was built. There is another impressive medieval doorway right at the south end which had been blocked but is now open for all to see, being the entrance to the modern visitor toilet block and, beyond that, the education centre and the song school. This is known as the Friends Building as it was financed completely by the Friends of Wells Cathedral.

Although the whole cloister rebuild occupied the best part of a century, the vaulting design (below) remained more or less the same, carried through from the east walk. It has an octagonal centre of liernes (small connecting ribs) in each bay with a variety of central bosses, some very worn and not easy to distinguish. The east and west cloister vaulting ribs spring directly from the capitals which are supported by elegant, ogee topped lozenge shapes. Both the east and west walks turn one bay into the south cloister; these bays acting as temporary buttresses as the south walk was the last to have been rebuilt.

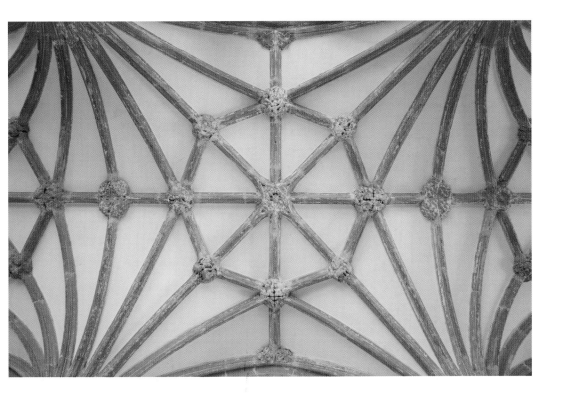

West Cloister

In the west walk there are many central roof bosses bearing either the arms, rebus or initials of Bishop Thomas Bekynton, even though he died about fifteen years before the cloister was completed in c.1480. In both the west and south walks, the inner wall as well as the outer was partially retained, the new fifteenth century inner wall sitting on the thirteenth century wall bench which acts as a kind of plinth. On the outer wall are several doors including the re-opened visitors' porch which is once again the main entrance into the cathedral for the lay community. The late medieval door north of this, now closed, was previously the entrance into the shop and restaurant which operated in this cloister until 2009. Facing this doorway on the wall bench on the left side, is the remains of the base of a thirteenth century blue lias shaft.

West cloister looking north

Continuing towards the west end of the cathedral, on the right is the opening into Palm Churchyard (the cloister garth) with a path running at a slant towards the east walk. A little further along also on the right is evidence of an opening, now glazed which might have been intended to link the west to the putative north walk. Opposite this on the south-west tower buttress facing into a possible north walk is a corbel head which appears to look towards the east walk. Moving towards the south, a glance inside the visitors' porch reveals two more doors, one of which opens onto a staircase which leads to the upper storey. This storey, built to mirror the east cloister library was originally occupied by the grammar school, a choristers' practice room and probably lodgings for the school master. Today it is occupied by offices and the more modern archives with an office for the archivist and an archive reading room.

When the present east and west cloisters were completed, pitched ridge roofs replaced the pentices and at the south end of each, on the ridge, is a finial; on the east ridge of a stone lion (right) and on the west a creature which is so worn that it is impossible to determine exactly what it is! Both can best be seen from Palm Churchyard.

South Cloister

The last cloister to be rebuilt is different from the other two in several ways. Although the vault still has a central octagonal shape, the ribs spring from small foliate capitals. This walk never had an upper storey but a pitched roof replaced the pentice to match the other two cloisters. If approached from the west cloister one bay of the south walk still has the arms of Bekynton. It is the second bay in, where the south cloister build ended, construction having started from the east (also the second bay). At the junction between Bekynton's bay and the end of the new south walk the vault rises by about 20 cm (8 in); the difference in height does not seem to be noticeable at the east end. There are more varied designs in the central bosses of this walk: angels, Tudor roses, coats of arms including the royal arms and different foliage. Where the south build ends and meets Bekynton's turned bay there is a rather worn boss bearing the initials T. H. (Thomas Harris, treasurer of the cathedral) and the date 1508 in Arabic numerals (right), very difficult to define but important as it is considered to mark the completion of the whole fifteenth century cloister rebuild.

In all the cloisters there is much to look at in the shape of stone monuments, moved from the main body of the cathedral by Dean Goodenough in the 1840s. The exception to this is the Phelips memorial, now in the west cloister but previously in the St John the Baptist chapel. As it had only recently been placed there, the tactful dean left it, to be removed much later. Round the outer wall benches in the south cloister are examples of pieces of stone carving, a medieval stone coffin and other items of interest.

Palm Churchyard (the cloister garth)

This can be entered from the east or the west walk. If coming from the east, opposite the entrance is a metal peacock (Charles Hopkins 1969) on the outer wall; a symbol of immortality, beneath which on slate slabs are the names of those whose ashes are buried under the small wooden crosses in the churchyard. These are mainly prebendaries or canons of the cathedral.

Palm Churchyard is a tranquil place in which to wander. The screen walls with their traceries can be appreciated more fully from this side. Looking at the east wall, both in bays four and six, there are small pentices with entrances, now blocked up (late seventeenth century), from the east cloister. The pentices probably date from the time of Bishop Stillington (1466-1491) and mirror each other. The roofs of both these structures, gently sloping, are attached to the cloister at transom level. In bay six (the

The small pentices

furthest south), there is a discernible letter B in the left hand spandrel of the first arch; the right hand initial is lost. It is possible that the B is associated with Bekynton whom Stillington succeeded. The bay four pentices are later in style, being more Tudor in appearance; all four spandrels here are carved with ribbons.

There have been endless discussions over time concerning the use of these curious constructions; speculations such as 'lavatories' meaning a place of washing, a covered place for selling devotional candles, a place where linen is hung out to dry (Colchester) and others more far fetched. It is worth noting that the pentices flank the entrance to Stillington's Lady Chapel and that there must be a connection between them, the processional importance of the east cloister and the Lady Chapel itself. Possibly as Warwick Rodwell suggests they could have contained a small chantry altar each or indeed have been a sheltered spot from which to cense the graves in the churchyard during important liturgical processions.

The Dipping Place
Close to the pentices and convenient for access to water is the Dipping Place, now surrounded by iron railings, whereas previously a stone building surmounted it, as drawn by John Carter in 1794. The water flows from St

Andrew's Well through the medieval conduit which is aligned on the Anglo-Saxon cathedral, flowing almost diagonally across the cloister garth. The 'dipping well' (Rodwell) was built in the late twelfth or early thirteenth century and has had several alterations or rebuilds since. The stone steps were introduced in the middle of the fifteenth century, leading down to the water from the north. Although the steps and the conduit are very dark it is possible to hear, if not see, the water flowing down below. Because of two nineteenth century burials close to the western edge of the steps, a rather ugly wall of brick and concrete had to be built to support this side of the structure and the tombs above. The present re-constructed steps and railings belong to the early twentieth century. Again, there have been many discussions as to its use. Was it for washing liturgical linen; a latrine (this was quickly disproved); or just to supply water to the cathedral? This would have had great significance in the early Middle Ages as the supply comes directly from St Andrew's Well, whose purity was of symbolic and actual importance.

The dipping place from the inside

The churchyard has many graves and cannot therefore be excavated although it is known that the Anglo-Saxon cathedral crossed the cloister garth at almost the same angle as the conduit. In 1731/32 three yew trees were planted, one of which still grows in the centre of the garth. Cuttings from the yew trees were quite often used as a substitute for palms in the Palm Sunday Procession.

One curious piece of carved stone (left), the only one in the whole garth apart from those supporting the water spouts, can be found in the south-east corner of the south cloister. It is in fact situated above the buttress of the second bay from the east (the start of Stillington's involvement). It appears to be a boar with one tusk protruding from its slightly open mouth. Perhaps it is significant that the boar was an emblem of Richard III whose faithful adherent Stillington was and whose loyalty cost him his freedom.

The Camery

Entering the Camery by way of the east cloister, just beyond the archway is a comprehensive plan based on that of Warwick Rodwell to show the archaeological evidence of the previous buildings, investigated for the

The excavated Roman mausoleum

last time by him in 1978-80. The evolution of these buildings has been described in the first chapter, from the late Roman mausoleum, through the Anglo-Saxon mortuary chapel, the first Lady Chapel, the much enlarged Lady Chapel-by-the-Cloister, to the apse of the Anglo-Saxon cathedral itself. The last is just to the left of the entrance into the cloister; the rest of the ancient cathedral is buried under Palm Churchyard. What is evident is that all these buildings were at an angle 12° different from the present cathedral alignment. The only building at variance with this is the re-constructed base of Stillington's late fifteenth century Lady Chapel (marked in red on the plan), of which more later.

What of the Camery itself? It has always proved elusive to define the word 'camery'. It is almost certainly related to the word 'camera', a chamber and from there in its widest sense means some sort of enclosed space, often of considerable dimension. There is even to this day a bishop's camery and a church (cathedral) camery, divided probably in the early part of Bishop Jocelin's episcopate by the east wall of the present cathedral camery; it was and still is an important boundary between the bishop's own land and that of the cathedral. The oldest part is at the south end; there is a change of direction further north to enable the wall to skirt the present fourteenth century

Lady Chapel. This part of the wall was probably constructed even before the Lady Chapel was completed, almost exactly a century after the original wall. Being the oldest wall on the site, it has been much repaired and re-ordered over the centuries. Close examination reveals evidence of doors and windows, now blocked up (at least two of each). The only recess now evident is the 'hole in the wall' (right) where it is possible to see St Andrew's Well on the bishop's side of the divide. This window  has a surround of Doulting stone and dates from the fifteenth century; it is situated right over the medieval conduit which runs from St Andrew's Well, across the Camery and Palm Churchyard, and out into the market place (see archaeological plan at the Camery entrance).

The east wall used to extend further north than the flying buttress-arch where it now ends. The buttress-arch dates to around the mid fourteenth century and was built perhaps in part to provide extra support to the south-east corner of the Lady Chapel. It may be significant that from time to time springs erupted in the area east of the Lady Chapel, even quite close to it and therefore the buttress-arch also acted as a tell-tale in case these caused movement in the ground to the east.

The present iron gate which seals the Camery to the north was constructed in 1979; there had been a previous iron gate built in the late nineteenth century. Earlier still there was some kind of blocking wall with a small arched doorway, shown in a drawing by John Carter, which appears to be of early sixteenth century (Tudor) style. On the present gate at the top is a single shield of the cross of St Andrew and the inscription: RICHARD LEWIS: DEAN: 1990-2003. It was during his time as dean that the plans for modern buildings were first discussed and drafted and with which he was passionately involved. Only the endless time consumed in obtaining permissions prevented him from carrying out the work to its completion.

Standing now to face the east cloister, there are many tombs at the east end of the Camery; as early as 1243 it was designated as a cemetery for the vicars choral, in the area east of the old Lady Chapel-by-the-Cloister. The dominant outline of the re-constructed base of a large late fifteenth century Lady Chapel, shows the extent of the building instigated by Bishop Stillington (1466-1491). The old Lady Chapel-by-the-Cloister was pulled down to make way for a splendid late Gothic structure, intended also to be Stillington's mausoleum: his eternal resting place. To the right of this against the east cloister wall is the outline of the Holy Cross Chapel.

Impression of Stillington's Chapel drawn by Alan Rome

Despite Stillington's ideas of grandeur, his magnificent Lady Chapel existed not much more than half a century. It was certainly unusually large and judging from the stone remains, full of carvings and colour. A number of roof bosses still remain giving indication of elaborate fan-vaulting, and the panelling on the east cloister wall is part of what was the west wall of his chapel (pictured opposite). There were no windows in the west wall of the chapel at the time but a quatre-foil squint was inserted so that canons pacing up and down in the long gallery of the library above could see what was going on in the chapel. The two windows now flanking the squint were inserted in the mid sixteenth century. Since the chapel was sumptuous in every way, it is interesting that Stillington was almost never in Wells; just long enough to set the building works in motion as well as those of the south cloister. He is known to have visited briefly in 1476 when the treasurer, Dr Hugh Sugar, declared the old Lady Chapel-by-the-Cloister to be "ruinosa et defectiva"; this undoubtedly gave rise to the idea of a magnificent replacement.

Stillington was an ardent Yorkist and worked tirelessly for the cause. He was Lord Chancellor from 1467-1475 and served both Edward IV and Richard III. His downfall came after the defeat of Richard III at the Battle of Bosworth in 1485, when he was imprisoned in York, briefly pardoned and then imprisoned again in Windsor Castle where he died in May 1491. His earthly remains were buried in the chancel of his chapel in Wells and archaeology in the late 1970s revealed a tomb of substantial size. So much grave robbing had taken place that only some foot bones and a fibula remained (Rodwell).

It is known that the chapel was in use by 1488 but Edward VI's Chantries Act of 1547 spelled doom for this building, particularly as Lady Chapels

Discovered craters in chapel foundations

were distinctly unpopular with Protestants. Therefore in 1552, the king's agent Sir John Gate was granted the right to 'the Lady Chapel in the cloister on the south side of the cathedral with all stones, stonework, lead, glass, timber and iron; the said Sir John to clear the site of all rubbish, and make the ground fair and plain within the space of four ¼ years'. In compliance with this, the chapel was stripped of every moveable feature including paving, then partially blown up with gunpowder, strategically placed so that the columns crumbled and the great fan-vaulted ceiling fell into soft earth; hence many bosses survived. Warwick Rodwell's archaeological investigations found at least three craters where gunpowder had been placed.

Walking back towards the east cloister entrance, a glance at the outside of the south transept stair turret reveals a blocked door where Stillington's north transept (the north-west corner) was linked by a bridge to the

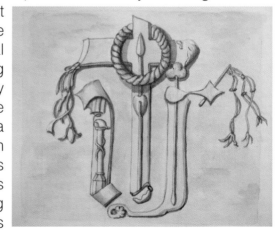

Drawing by Carlos of the sacred IHS monogram, 1824

cathedral. Turning left into the east cloister towards the exit, there are two large re-constructed central bosses on the wall bench belonging to Stillington's chapel. Immediately before that, in the first bay where there is a gap in the stone bench, is a much eroded IHS sacred monogram panel incorporating the instruments of the Passion. Because the features lack definition it is worth noting that several clarifying drawings were made of this, including one by John Carter in the 1790s.

In the final east walk bay is the re-opened medieval archway which was found to contain broken up stones from Stillington's chapel. Once an entrance to the Camery it now leads to the toilet block for visitors and further along, to the education area, two rooms with ample space for workshops to take place and for all the paraphernalia which this entails. It can also be used for adult lectures, particularly in the evening. The song school beyond it has two practice rooms, one capable of holding the entire choir, a music library and changing space for the vicars choral and the boy and girl choristers. This part is not open to the public and is secure for children's activities. Opposite the door into this area are more bosses from Stillington's chapel.

Before turning into the south cloister, and very much off centre as already mentioned, is the bishop's door and archway of the early thirteenth century; a statue of St Andrew is above the arch, on the right (pictured below). The door, which now opens inwards, originally opened outwards, probably onto some kind of porch. The door was most likely re-hung when the wicket door was cut in, in the sixteenth century. Nowadays a glass door enables visitors to glimpse the gate house and moat of the bishop's palace during the daytime.

Passing along the south cloister and part of the west walk, the exit is back towards the entrance cloister where the one-way system obliges visitors to turn left towards an attractively stocked shop, past the tranquil Mary Mitchell garden and the stairs to the 'Chapter two' restaurant. Outside the wall is Bishop Bekynton's Penniless Porch to the left, and to the right is the Cathedral Green and an impressive row of medieval houses, for the canons, opposite the cathedral.

Penniless Porch from the marketplace

Chapter 9
Cathedral Precinct and North Façade

The Green

In medieval times this was a lay burial ground from 1243 when an avenue of elms was planted; perhaps another landscaping recorded in 1725-1731 may have ended this use, although it went on being called a churchyard until 1808. The three gates which close off what is now Cathedral Green and the cathedral precinct were all built by Bishop Bekynton: Penniless Porch with its shelter for beggars, and Brown's Gate, so called simply because the lease to it and the house to the south was held by Richard Brown, a shoemaker, in 1553; both these gates were constructed in the 1450s; the Chain Gate at the east end came later. The area within these gates, together with the block of houses to the north, defined the limits of the jurisdiction of the Dean and Chapter and was known as the Liberty. It was separate from the city and exempt from its taxes and even those of the bishop (Meek). The street now called The Liberty was included in this and it is still graced with very fine houses, many now part of Wells Cathedral School.

Facing the north side of Cathedral Green with Brown's Gate on the left is a row of substantial medieval canonical houses. Archaeological evidence indicates that there were some canonical houses as far back as the twelfth century, but no trace of these remains to be seen. The first house east of Brown's Gate is No. 6 Cathedral Green, which is built low and embattled, the present structure dating from the fifteenth to sixteenth centuries (Pevsner). It has a crenellated porch and a projecting polygonal turret. Many alterations have taken place over the centuries including new windows c.1780-1800. Next door to this is No. 7 which on the face of it is a fine late Georgian house and which has lost, even on the inside, all traces of its medieval predecessor except a very thick, now interior wall which is probably the remains of the medieval back wall of the house. The Grecian Doric porch is c.1820s. Both these houses are now in private hands.

The Old Deanery

In medieval times this was the Deanery, the residence of the dean until half-way through the twentieth century. It is an imposing building and reflects the importance of the status of the dean in the middle ages and beyond. Like all the other buildings on the north side of the Green, it has been substantially altered over the centuries. The first mention of the present building is in 1236; it then consisted of four ranges around an inner court, now filled in with later additions, leaving only a light-well.

The Old Deanery facing the Green

The most dramatic alterations were carried out by Dean Gunthorpe (1472-1498), a statesman and scholar who was friend both to Edward IV and Henry VII. He greatly enlarged and enriched the north range and his rebus (a gun) appears all over this wing together with Edward IV's 'rose-en-soleil'. The story that he built it especially for a visit from Henry VII is most likely untrue; he probably had it built to give himself more sumptuous living quarters. There is no doubt however that Henry VII was his guest both in 1491 and again in 1497 and profited from the new luxurious surroundings. The architect is thought to have been William Smyth, cathedral master mason c.1480-1490. Following centuries saw many alterations both inside and out, including turning one medieval hall into small rooms. The outside facing the Green appears to be more of the eighteenth century because of a complete replacement of the windows. Since the 1960s when it became the Old Deanery, it has been home to the diocesan offices and the interior was altered once again to make it fit for purpose. The dean at the time, Christopher Woodforde, could no longer afford the upkeep of such a large establishment and subsequently moved into Vicars' Close. His successor Dean Edwards took up residence in the Liberty—a house still in use by the dean and still called the Dean's Lodging, because it was never meant to be permanent.

The latest alteration to the Old Deanery is the development of the garden to the north which had been much neglected and left to its own devices. This present garden (pictured above), originally much larger, was probably the dean's walled garden, his private space accessible only from the house. In 2003 a group of enthusiastic volunteers banded together to re-create a modern version of Dean William Turner's garden. Dean Turner (1551-1554; 1560-1568) as already mentioned in connection with the library, was a keen proponent of herbal medicine and was the author of the first English Herbal. Over the years this idea of re-creating the garden has evolved and flourished. It is of the Tudor period, in a style which Turner would have recognized, and is full of plants which he had described in his writings. Replacing ugly concrete, there are now geometric gravel cross-paths in Tudor style; a fern and woodland area with a blanket of wild cyclamen in autumn; and medieval roses flourish on the east rampart. There are period fruit trees in a little orchard and many varied herbs in the 'chequer beds' which flank the porch.

Dean Gunthorpe's wing

Then there is the Italian courtyard, a tranquil spot with its lion's head fountain, in which to sit and contemplate the splendours of Dean Gunthorpe's wing. Turner had a great affinity to Italy as he had studied botany and medicine with the best Italian teachers and when he was expelled from the Deanery by Catholic Mary Tudor, he used his exile to renew his contacts in Italy and Germany. As a Doctor of Medicine he apparently still practised his profession while exercising the office of dean.

Each year the variety of plants, all carefully researched, increases; the project continues to be self-funding and totally reliant on its dedicated team of volunteers.

The gardens can be visited on advertised Open Days in spring, summer and autumn and in addition are open on Wednesday afternoons in June, July and August (1.30-3.00 p.m.) Admission is free but donations are always gratefully accepted.

Wells Museum

The next canonical house east of the Old Deanery was known as the chancellor's residence, although over the centuries many others lived there too. There is no longer any trace of the medieval house but the earliest tenant dates back to Bishop Burnell's episcopate: a certain Richard de Kennilworth who took up residence in 1286. Perhaps one of the most well-known occupants was Robert Stillington (bishop 1466-1491), when he was chancellor to Bishop Bekynton. By the time Thomas Cornish was given the house in the late fifteenth century it was described as 'broken down and ruinous and unfit for habitation'. He was therefore given permission to live in the hospital of St John the Baptist, of which he was prior. His tomb near the chapter house steps has been mentioned in chapter 4.

The core of the house as it is today is sixteenth century (Tudor) but various updates, including seventeenth century windows, culminated in a comprehensive restoration in the Regency Gothic style c.1828. The house was taken over in 1928 by the trustees of Wells Museum, having previously been occupied by the headmaster of the Cathedral School.

Wells Cathedral Music School

The next canonical house to the east was the residence of the archdeacon of Wells; it is now used by the Cathedral School as a concert hall and a place for ensembles to practise. Bishop Jocelin was first given this house for one of his canons (Bailey). The present building was constructed for Archdeacon Andrew Holes (1450-1470) and there are many interesting features of this period still in existence, such as the timber roof of the great

hall: the part now used as a concert hall (right). This roof has collar beams, four tiers of wind-braces, and a deeply undercut frieze with blind arcading above. Noticeable also is a cinque-cusped arch with thirteenth century mouldings, now blocked in and serving as a recess, and a cusped thirteenth century lancet survives low down in the north wall to the west of this. Other features from the past are the battlements and two angle-turrets, one at either end of the façade, similar to those in the Old Deanery. On the east gable end are three blocked doors originally leading into the kitchen, pantry and buttery. In the nineteenth century a great deal of alteration and restoration took place under the direction of Edmund Buckle (1888-1889). The outside suffered much interference and within the hall itself it was Buckle who inserted the limed oak fittings, staircase and gallery, when it became the Theological College library.

The last archdeacon to occupy this house was Polydore Virgil (1508-1555), who, although he was Italian, is best known for his twenty-seven volume History of England. During his time as archdeacon he acted for several of his compatriots as agent, including Cardinal Hadrian de Costello, bishop of Bath and Wells who, if he ever visited England at all, only came very briefly.

Following this the house had a chequered career as an assembly and banqueting room followed by its use as the Old City Brewery. In the late 1880s it was sold to the trustees of Wells Theological College for which it provided a library (the hall), lecture room and common room. When the college transferred to Salisbury it was acquired by Wells Cathedral School to serve as its concert hall and office space for the music department.

It is possible for visitors to see the interior of the hall as during term time there are lunchtime concerts at least twice a week, which are free and open to the public (normally Tuesdays and Thursdays: 1.00-1.30 p.m.).

The Tower House
Continuing past Vicars' Hall and the entrance to the Close is another canonical house, known as the Tower House by virtue of a tower at the north-east end, probably built in the sixteenth century. This was the residence of the precentor from 1338-1734. The main range of the building running north to south is early fourteenth century. There is a two-light decorated window with transom in the south gable; this is now blocked. Originally this house had a first floor hall with an undercroft at the south end. Still existing is the roof with two tiers of wind-braces and in the south-east angle is a spiral staircase leading up the stair turret.

In 1338, Bishop Ralph of Shrewsbury had granted to 'William de Littleton, and to his successors in the precentorship the house….with a garden adjoining', all this for a fine of 20s., payable to the Dean and Chapter (Sherwin Bailey). Thomas Boleyn (whose tomb may be the fine alabaster in St Calixtus Chapel) who was precentor between 1451 and 1472 also lived in this house. The last precentor to occupy the premises was Dr Robert Creyghton II who held office 1674-1734 when he died at the age of ninety six. It is no accident that the precentor's house was next to Vicars' Close, where the men of the choir who were in his care, were housed. This house is now in private hands.

In more modern times, the novelist Elizabeth Goudge was born in the house but moved across the road to the Rib at the age of two when her father became principal of the Theological College. Her association with the house did not end there as the next occupants were the family of the new vice principal of the college Canon Hollis, who came to have four sons who proved to be excellent playmates for Elizabeth. Elizabeth's mother was a permanent invalid so the Tower House across the road was a haven of joy and friendship for this only child. The house was famously included in two of her books: *City of Bells* (based on Wells) and the less well-known *Sister of the Angels*.

The Rib

Opposite this on the south side of St Andrew's Street is the house (above) known as the Rib; so called because it was in the gift of the bishop, as were four other houses now lost. Collectively these were known as the bishop's ribs. This Rib is on a site occupied since c.1130, pre-dating the present cathedral. The existing house has elements from the fourteenth century but its gabled east-west range is mid fifteenth century and may have been built by Bishop Bekynton. Over the porch is a three light window with traceries similar to those of the Chain Gate, also built by Bekynton; this design is not found anywhere else. Underneath this window are three tournament shields, similar to smaller versions on the entrance to Vicars' Close but more precisely on the house now known as No. 14 within the Close, next to the chapel. One of these tournament shields has a W, which may refer to Canon Walter Osborne (1464-1484). This part originally had a double height hall and the fifteenth century roof is still largely intact. It consists of six bays, four tiers of wind-braces and wall shafts in the two corners which are carried by stone angel corbels. Over the porch is a small oratory whose glass shows a seraph and Canon Osborne's initials (dated c.1470). The house also boasts a very fine garden which merges into the garden of the Bishop's Palace. Now in private ownership, it was previously occupied by the headmaster of Wells Cathedral School.

Cathedral North Porch

From here proceeding westwards, passing under the Chain Gate, the magnificent north porch of the cathedral can be seen in all its splendour. It is the most luxurious of the cathedral's entrances as it was the door used by the canons when coming in for services, especially for the 'quinque personae', the dignitaries who made up the Dean and Chapter.

Exterior Construction
The sides of the porch to east and west are very plain so that all interest is focussed on the front. The gable is flanked by tall polygonal pinnacles placed on top of the buttresses on either side to add weight to support the structure as well as being decorative. Within the gable are three small stepped lancet windows which light the room above the porch. These are set centrally within six blind lancets decorated with small pieces of sculpture. Where the east side of the porch meets the north aisle outer wall, are three slit windows which were there to shed light on a staircase used by the masons to access the floor above. The doorway into this staircase is just inside the north nave aisle, on the

left of the entrance. The main part of the staircase has long since been blocked; the base of it is used by the virgers for the storage of candles.

The main arched doorway is strikingly carved with a complicated chevron-based design (left) similar to that found in the ruined Lady Chapel at Glastonbury Abbey. This design alternates with plain rounded arcs which blend with the rounded columns below. All the free-standing shafts at the side were originally of blue lias, echoing the construction of the west front; the last one being removed by master mason 'Bert' Wheeler in 1956. These columns form a distinctive pattern giving perspective, light and shade to the entrance and end in two columns facing inwards. They are topped by finely carved capitals. On the left are five carved images of the martyrdom of St Edmund (king of Anglia). He is shown pierced by many arrows, shot by the invading Danes from both sides. He then appears bowing his crowned head, humbly awaiting execution and the final image is of a wolf, retrieving the severed head from the forest and presenting it to the king's followers to be reunited with his body. Jerry Sampson thinks this series might have been carved by Adam Lock himself. On the right there is no story, but simply stiff-leafed foliage possibly indicating the hurried end of a building phase.

The martyrdom of St Edmund

Above the archway are two square panels of unequal size (pictured overleaf). The one on the left shows David rescuing a lamb from the jaws of a lion, symbolizing Christ redeeming mankind, and on the right is a winged griffin, half eagle, half lion: an allegory of the Christ, the lion symbolizing his

159

strength and the eagle his wisdom. All this foretells what is portrayed in the interior of the porch as well as foreshadowing the imagery of the west front.

The style of the porch according to Sampson is experimental, possibly similar to that of the thirteenth century cloisters where still existing spandrels show a similarity in style. The main part of the building had to exhibit homogeneity and harmony over decades of construction so that any advance in style of a more innovative nature had to be practised in outer-lying areas where it did not impinge on the uniformity of the interior.

The porch was probably finished by 1205/6; certainly it was functioning by 1207 when Nicholas of Wells 'gives to the church of St Andrew and to Bishop Jocelin houses and land before the great gate of the canons (ante magnam portam canonicorum)'. During the long break in the building c.1208-1220, the porch would have assisted in buttressing the completed work up to north aisle triforium level, of phase four of the building campaign (i.e. the east nave to the mid nave break).

Interior
The outer doors of the porch were added in 1725/6 and are similar in style to those in the interior entrance to the two western towers. In the 1930s they were repaired and turned around by 'Bert' Wheeler, so that when the doors are closed, the original inner face is revealed on the outside. The other door into the cathedral itself is thirteenth century but was later re-faced with fifteenth century ornament and tracery. The small wicket door was cut in during the 1930s.

The porch consists of two bays and has a stone bench on both sides. There are eight shallow niches above each bench, with fine foliate spandrel carvings. Above these are string courses which are being eaten up by dragon-like monsters from either side (pictured opposite); the same idea is found in the Bristol Elder Lady Chapel (was this also Adam Lock?). Above the string courses are six deeply recessed niches on either side with delicate interlacing arches also to be found on the west front. These niches with their free-standing columns were designed, according to Jerry Sampson, to hold free-standing sculptures of a considerable size; possibly the twelve apostles again foretelling the west front. If this was the case then the niche now blocked up above the inner doorway could well have been the figure of Christ in Majesty. Below this niche on either side of the doorway, in the corners, are two sculpted figures. On the left is a canon with a scroll bearing the text, 'intra in gaudium domini tui' (enter into the joy of thy Lord. Matthew 25 v. 21). On the right is a bishop with his hand raised in blessing. Above the evidently focal middle tier of niches are four shallow ones on the east and west with a metal grid across and some spikes to deter roosting pigeons. These have always been a menace in the past and even now accept the challenge of finding an unprotected abacus or two on which to perch.

Generally speaking the north porch would appear to be a masons' experimental opportunity, in particular for sculpture, to prepare for the exciting spectacle of the west front.

String course dragons

The Tracing Floor
The room above the porch lit by the three lancet windows is a rarity in that it is one of only two medieval tracing floors of this type in the country, the other one being at York.

Arnold Pacey, who has made a critical study of tracing floors and medieval technical drawings in general, thinks that the York floor came first and that the idea filtered down to Wells: using a covering of gypsum to scratch with wire or compass point, or draw with chalk or charcoal, designs of particular areas of building. The tracing floor at Wells is damaged partly by having been used for a short while in the nineteenth century as a school room; heavy desks and table legs have pitted the floor and there are signs of furniture being dragged. Consequently, 'there is hardly a single drawing that is not interrupted by damage to the surface' (Pacey).

The gypsum floor

Most of the drawings which survive at least in part, can be dated to c.1420 although it is possible that the floor was laid a hundred years before, roughly when the parapets had been inserted round the east and west sides of the porch and the rest of the building. The drawings are not easy to interpret as many are superimposed on others. Linzee Colchester was sure that a surviving ogee arch was the design for windows in Vicars' Close but it is now evident, through Pacey's careful measurements, that this arch relates to the tracery of the inner screen of the east cloister. Other lines and designs have also been interpreted as belonging to the east cloister, including part of the vault with its octagonal lierne centre.

What seems probable since Pacey's study is that these gypsum floors were not necessarily for the cutting out of moulds or templates, but a place for experimental drawing combining elements from elevations and sections in one plan, and that much of the Wells tracing floor shows the detail of one complete sample bay of the east cloister of the fifteenth century re-build. Any larger construction would have been designed on the ground.

Since after this period the masons went away and the staircase was blocked, the only access now is by way of the triforium. It is not generally open to the public but can be seen as part of a specially booked tour of the upper levels of the cathedral.

Sculpture
Outside the north porch are four sculptures depicting the symbols of the four evangelists: the winged man of St Matthew, the winged lion of St Mark, the ox of St Luke and the eagle of St John. These were carved by Mary Spencer

Watson (d.2006) in Portland stone. The designs are based on the Book of Kells. They were installed in 1995 and were a gift from the Jerusalem Trust.

The Outside Clock

Moving to the east, on the wall of the north transept is a clock dial flanked by two armed knights whose duty it is to strike the quarter hours. The style of their armour defines the date of the clock. This clock which can be seen from a small window opposite (towards the Chain Gate) was placed there in the second half of the 1400s to remind the Vicars Choral of their duty to be on time for cathedral services. The clock faces the entrance to their dining hall from the kitchen where one of their number would have to keep an eye on the time.

This clock is worked by the same mechanism as the more ancient interior one, as is the great bell in a corner pinnacle of the central tower which gives the hour to the citizens of Wells. In the 1800s the dial was repainted as a twelve hour clock (previously it was twenty four hours) with gilt black letter Roman numerals. In the four corners of the face are the symbols of the four evangelists. Between the armoured knights is a Latin text: 'NEQUID PEREAT' (let nothing be lost). This probably refers to the losing of time: a warning, to the Vicars Choral perhaps, to be scrupulous in their prompt attendance at services.

The Chain Gate

Chapter 10
The Chain Gate, Vicars' Hall and Close

Chain Gate

Looking eastwards from the clock, the outline of the Chapter House steps can be seen, leading upwards to the Chain Bridge which spans the road between the north side of the Cathedral and Vicars' Hall.

The bridge with gate beneath was built by Bishop Bekynton at his own expense of 500 marks between March 1459 and February 1460, when the vicars recorded their thanks to the bishop on its completion. No longer did they have to dodge wagons clattering down the hill or importunate people or indeed inclement weather while crossing the road. They were now safe to pass unhindered between their Hall and their business in the cathedral quire and chapels.

The gate itself is an imposing perpendicular structure with ornate carving, now very much worn by weather and time. On the east side of the gate where it joins the Hall there is a small square addition to the structure, built certainly during Bekynton's lifetime as it bears his coat of arms. This was to avoid the vicars, in the original straight construction, entering directly into the buttery section of their Hall; temptation to indulge was great! A dog-leg structure was therefore swiftly added so that the entrance came into a screens passage to the east of the buttery.

The Vicars' Hall

Construction

Facing the Vicars' Hall on either side of the Chain Gate and looking down the Close, it is evident that the whole complex was built on the plot of one

Looking up Vicars' Close through the archway

medieval canonical house and garden. At the time, when Bishop Ralph of Shrewsbury (1329-1363) wanted to house the vicars communally, this house in the gift of the bishop was nominally occupied by Canon Alan de Hothum who by the late 1340s was absent, living in London and acting as official receiver of monies for the Papal Nuncio.

Two previous attempts to provide a community for the vicars had come to nothing but Bishop Ralph was determined to protect his young clerks and to provide them with communal dining facilities and kitchen and a single house for each, enclosed against the town by a high wall. The Vicars' Hall itself (that is, the first storey) was almost certainly extended above what had been the hall of the canonical house. To the west of the Chain Gate, the ground floor is now occupied by the cathedral offices and had originally been cellar and storage space. Above, the roof-line is raised at the western end and it is clear that the original building has been extended. This happened in the 1860s when John Henry Parker, an antiquarian and architect from Oxford, built this extension and made considerable alterations to the inside. On the outside facing west, he placed an oriel window which is a copy of the original, now in No 1 St Andrew's Street. Also, at eye level on the south side is a recycled piece of Norman open chevron stone incorporated in a now closed archway.

Eastwards from the Chain Gate looking north are the two archways which give entrance to Vicars' Close: the smaller one for pedestrians and the larger for vehicles. These are not part of the original structure but were carved out of the two final bays of the ground floor hall. The original small pedestrian entrance to the east is now incorporated into No 1 St Andrew Street, then the first house in the Close. The exact date of the two present arches had been a puzzle until Anne Crawford (archivist) found an entry in the vicars' accounts of c.1421 (VC/F1/1-2): 'And in the repair of the great gate at the entry of the Close, 4d.' This would place it within the building phase of the present staircase leading from the Close to the Hall above and also ultimately to the building of the chapel at the far end. Above the gates are modified windows of late 15th or early 16th century design on both the north and south sides.

The Offices

Entering the ground floor on the west side to visit the cathedral offices and continuing through to what is now the chapter room and was originally cellar and storage space for the vicars, there is evidence of some thirteenth century features of the original ground floor hall, such as the columns which probably supported a wooden vault, the hall being just one tall storey at this time (Rodwell). The chapter room (right), which is underneath the present Hall, consists of four bays and has many of J. H. Parker's modifications, including a large fireplace and an ornate ceiling decorated by William Burges whom he employed. Some Burges decoration is also on the ceilings of the offices to the west, (his extension) and indeed in No 22 Vicars' Close where Parker lived for a while. It is thought that the fourth bay of the chapter room might have been a porter's lodge as a small door opens onto the entrance to the Close. Beyond that in the space now occupied by the entrance arches, there was perhaps the first chapel used by the vicars for their private worship.

The Hall

Coming now to the Vicars' Hall, it can be entered by an imposing straight staircase rising from inside the Close. This present staircase was built in the 1420s with a covering storey above added at around this time to house the administrative rooms of the College of Vicars Choral; the other entrance is by way of the chapter house steps and across the Chain Bridge. Bishop Ralph had handed over the hall buildings by the end of 1348. In November of that year Alice Swansee, mother of Philip, a vicar choral who had predeceased her, left in her will a large brass vessel, a basin with ewer,

Vicars' Hall looking east

and a table for their Hall, 'for the use of the Vicars ... dwelling in the new building which the Bishop has built.' Edward III's licence in mortmain was dated 3 December 1348. Bishop Ralph's deed of gift, the vicars' charter, was dated 30 December 1348, endorsed by the Prior and Chapter of Bath on 1 January 1349 and by the Dean and Chapter of Wells on 3 January 1349. 1348/49 was the year when the Black Death was virulent in Somerset and it is known that almost half the clergy died. Consequently the houses of the Close were not completed, though under construction, for some considerable time.

Entering the Hall itself, there would have been a screens passage after the construction of Bishop Bekynton's Chain Bridge, linking the two entrances to the Hall. To the west of this was the buttery and on the south wall can still be seen the remains of original window mullions: all that was left after the Chain Bridge was built. The first entrance to the Hall was covered in when the already mentioned dog-leg was made. The window high in the west wall was inserted because that end of the Hall was very dark, having lost two windows. They needed to be able to find the vats of ale! When repairs were made to this window in 1973, recycled sections of two mullions from the destroyed windows were found to have been used.

There are still three of the early windows in situ, typical of William Joy's design, who as master mason (1329-1348) was responsible for the building of the scissor arches in the Cathedral. His recognizable two-light, traceried and transomed windows with wave mouldings still contain within the traceries some medieval glass: St Margaret on the south and St Katherine with her wheel on the north with possibly St Hugh in the adjacent one. The two oriel windows at the eastern end, on either side, were put in place by Richard Pomeroy, a wealthy vicar choral and also Keeper of the Fabric from 1488 to 1514. He is immortalized in the tracery on the north side as the donor, dressed in blue, and the arms of St Andrew encompassed with his name are in the south-east corner of the east wall. He was probably also responsible for the plainer oriel window at the western end of the north wall and he may even have constructed the present plastered, barrel-vaulted

The Vicar's Hall tracery: (L-R) St Katherine, Richard Pomeroy, and St Margaret

ceiling; this consists of nine and a half bays with plain chamfered ribs. Within this structure, on either side of the door on the north, there are still traces of where the screens were originally fixed.

Pomeroy's considerable contribution to the Hall is also remembered in a carved inscription on the mantel-shelf of the Tudor fireplace. Loosely translated from the Latin, it says, "Pray for the soul of Richard Pomeroy whom God save." There has been much discussion as to the initials in the upper corners of the fireplace, which are now taken to be K.S. Who this was is a matter for conjecture. The present fireplace was probably rebuilt from an existing one and incorporates a lectern or pulpit high up within the window embrasure so that a member of the vicars choral could read to his silent colleagues during meal times.

The plaster walls are clad with panelling, some medieval and possibly original (plain oak with v-jointed edges), on part of both the north and south sides. On the east wall is later, linenfold panelling, not seen in England until Henry VIII's reign. Some of the rails are decorated with sphinx-like creatures and other Renaissance ornamentation. Above this panelling are two wooden figures (left and right), which without a doubt, by the style of their curved bodies, are contemporary with the Hall. These figures, beautifully carved with some paint still visible are usually taken to represent either the Annunciation or the Visitation. Opinion seems to be more or less equally divided. Both figures rest on corbels, the one on the north depicts the three kings offering gifts and on the south shows two boys wrestling, reputed to be Jesus and his cousin, John the Baptist. These figures doubtless lent a certain grandeur to the high table area.

Between these two figures there now hangs a historic painting of the vicars choral; originally it hung on the wall of the Close staircase and then was removed in the nineteenth century to hang inside, over the fireplace. Its present position enhances the focus on the east end. It was placed there after conservation work in 2007. It depicts the history of the three charters giving the vicars their independence as a college: Bishop Ralph (1348), Bishop Bekynton (1459) and Elizabeth I (1591). The painting is intriguing and there is much speculation as to how old it really is. Is the bishop in the top left hand corner presenting the charter Bishop Ralph or an over-painted Bishop Bekynton? Certainly the surpliced vicars, kneeling to present their petition are older and more primitive in style than those on the right, who are much larger and distinctly Elizabethan with their ruffs and bearded faces. It is also known that the faces of these particular vicars were heavily over-painted during restoration in the nineteenth century, when it was also reframed under the direction of Arthur du Cane (priest vicar) in 1862.

In the bottom left hand corner is a stone tablet giving a doggerel Latin account of the giving of Elizabeth's charter as a consummation of the other two; both bishops are mentioned by name. The bishop holding his charter and the vicars presenting their petition also have doggerel Latin verse describing their purpose. These were first translated by Godwin, an antiquarian, in 1601. Godwin implied that the 1591 version of the painting probably concealed an earlier one. Even after Helen White's conservation and cleaning in 2007 it is impossible to prove that it is older than 1591. She did reveal lower layers of paint on the ruffs, for example, but these were so thin and delicate that further investigation might have destroyed them. As the painting is on wood, dendrochronology was also attempted but the wood was cut so as to make dating impossible as there were not enough rings. This was a brave attempt to tackle the mystery of its age, all the more so as previously, in 1968, the Victoria and Albert Museum had decided not to investigate because of the fragility of the paint layers. The nineteenth century restorers did not help matters by adding a thick coat of protective varnish.

Opposite, against the west wall, is a piece of contemporary furniture: the very large bread cupboard (right), big enough to hold bread rations for forty two men. Although this is much worn in places, it is nevertheless remarkable that it has survived at all. Some of the older furniture now stands on the Chain Bridge to make room for modern tables and chairs for the use of catering enterprises. There are several medieval benches, not specifically dated, and two fine Restoration tables. John Henry Parker's 1860s dresser is on the north wall.

The medieval kitchen can be entered down some steps from a skewed doorway to the left of the bread cupboard. Unfortunately, very little of the original features can be seen. They are virtually obliterated by equipment and furniture belonging to the commercial catering arm of the cathedral. On the west side is the fireplace with its spit still fixed in place and somewhere in one corner is the stone sink, carved from a single block. This would have stood on supports above a drain, still to be seen, running north to south in the floor, where the water could run out through a chute fixed in a hole in the wall, on to any unsuspecting passers-by below. Originally, there was a brass cauldron or cooking pot also hanging in the fireplace. This was removed for safe keeping to the muniment room in the cathedral library. A 1348 description of this area also mentions a bake-house of which there is now no sign. West of the medieval kitchen is Parker's extension, modernized and still used as a functioning kitchen to supply lunches and dinners in the Hall by arrangement.

The Treasury Block

Facing the exit door to the Close, two smaller doors can be seen. The one on the left, part of the medieval design, houses a staircase to gain immediate access to the cellar to enable replenishing of the kitchen and buttery stores. On the right, where there may have been a recessed cupboard, is the door, leading by way of a short spiral staircase to the rooms built around 1420-1430. The first room is the chequer where the vicars' annually elected receiver took in rents and other dues from tenants of their gradually accumulated estates. At the top of the stair, built into the structure, is a cupboard where writing implements were kept and opposite is a piscina, complete with drainage holes and hook for a ewer, where the receiver could wash his inky fingers. Also on this wall is a large fireplace, probably much enlarged in Tudor times. It was a very cold place to work in as only wooden shutters, still in place, served to keep out the cold. This room was not glazed until c.1912. The oak roof is striking and full of elaborate detail with a frieze of blind trefoil arcading and two tiers of wind-braces. There are several examples of this in houses of the same period. On the far wall to the north is a chest dated 1633 with a heart-shaped ornamentation, typical Somerset work of that time. Inside is a tray in which to keep official seals and a large space for books, papers and rolls.

The chequer, looking through to the muniment room

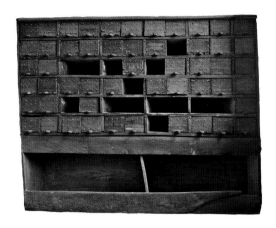

Through the doorway is a small room situated in the tower at the foot of the Close staircase. This was the muniment room, for keeping documents. It houses a medieval multi-drawer armoire (above), the equivalent of a modern filing cabinet. It is contemporary with the building. Designed to take rolls, possibly leases of properties; it originally had 72 drawers, with storage space underneath. Each drawer has a finger-tab for easy opening and brass pins with decorated heads to fix parchment labels. There is a large window looking out onto the Close.

In the south-east corner is a small spiral stair lit by a very narrow slit window leading down to the treasury. Beneath it is a thick stone vault for greater security, paid for by the vicars themselves in 1448. This is the roof of the tower porch and can be examined from below in the Close. A section of the timber floor in the muniment room can be lifted up to lower larger objects down. A long iron bar could also be dropped from a hole in this floor through three rings, across the treasury door below as an effective bolting mechanism. In the treasury room itself, is another armoire with ten cupboards. The tall upper cupboards were probably for best vestments of exceptional quality and the smaller ones below for mass vessels and some plate. Some of the locks are still in place. This room also has one very narrow slit window, impossible even for a child to access from the outside. Security was complete.

View of the Close from the muniment room

Vicars' Close looking south

The Vicars' Close

Looking down the Close from the gateway (south) end it seems to be longer than it really is, tapering into the distance. Some thought that this was a deliberate creation of a false perspective but it now seems more likely that the space at the north end, 2.7 metres narrower than the south, was simply dictated by the size of the available plot, which though ostensibly rectangular had to fit in with the boundaries on either side. Nowadays it looks like a street but when built, much more resembled an Oxbridge college quadrangle, with a narrow path running around the perimeter of the Close. The shape changed because the vicars in the early 1400s decided that front gardens would be an agreeable addition. Walls were built to define their plots, then 1.8m high but now considerably lower. Each had a stone arched gateway of which only five remain. This development was probably during Bishop Bubwith's time (1407-1424). In Bishop Ralph's construction there were forty-two houses for forty-two vicars choral (twenty-two on the east and twenty on the west), each with a central chimney and a one up one down arrangement, although it is highly probable that on each floor there was a smaller room separated by a screen. Each house had a staircase projection at the back, incorporated into which was a latrine on the ground floor and possibly even on the floor above. A main drain was situated immediately beyond the end wall with shafts from the latrines discharging into it. After the Reformation, when vicars were allowed to marry, thirty of the houses were doubled, leaving only twelve single ones. This arrangement can still be seen today, as well as many adjustments to windows and doors and, unseen, various extensions on the back.

The house that most resembles the original bachelor lodgings is No 22 (right). This was last restored in 1991 enabling more detailed examination of the structure. Looking at the façade, it is the only house with unaltered windows. This is one of the houses acquired by John Henry Parker (also Nos. 27 and 28 and Vicars Hall) in the 1860s. In the downstairs hall or main room the ceiling was decorated by William Burges for Parker, as it was also in No 28.

Although there were changes throughout the centuries the nineteenth century saw major alterations such as sash-windows and extensive

re-roofing, after a period of neglect. Perhaps however, the most remarked on feature is the tall octagonal chimney shafts, added to the original bases of the stacks, erected after the death of Bishop Bekynton by his executors. Bekynton's arms and those of the See alternate in the base of the stack while just below the eaves course are the arms of his executors; Hugh Sugar, Richard Swan and John Pope (Talbot), which succeed each other in sequence. In Tudor times, an extension was built to No 14 in the form of a shallow wing joining the house to the chapel. Its façade is extravagantly decorated with four tournament shields, one of which has the arms of Bishop Stillington (1465-91) thereby dating the work to c.1480-1490. Interestingly, similar shields occur on the main archway of the Close in miniature, under the oriel window on the south side and also on the porch of the house known as the Rib diagonally opposite Vicars Hall. In around 1670 two breaches were made in the north wall separating the Close from the Liberty to allow access to the road behind, thus opening up the other end of the Close.

Despite all the alterations both inside and out, a small amount of decorative medieval polychrome can still be found, such as the remains of scrollwork and fleur-de-lys coloured red, in No 9 and a fifteenth century painting of stylized vegetation in No 23. The houses do not appear to have been uniform and several teams of masons were probably at work. It is certain that all the houses were finished by the time of Bishop Ralph's death in 1363 as in his will dated 12th May of that year, he leaves grain and livestock 'to the vicars of Wells dwelling in the houses built by me.' This seems to suggest that all was complete.

Chapel and Library

Only the chapel building (opposite) was constructed later, in the early fifteenth century, probably during the episcopates of Bishops Bubwith and Stafford. It was then that the whole site was finally enclosed, the only entrance being, at that stage, on the south side. The building has two storeys with a parapet and is not much larger than the vicars' houses. The entrance is in the south-west corner, the door being rather awkwardly situated underneath a window opening. This oak door is original and the four wooden shields bear the arms of The See of Bath and Wells, Bishop Bubwith, Bishop Stafford and the Hungerford family (Bekynton bought their manor of Shipham to support the vicars choral); all were expressly concerned with the welfare of the men. Apart from the crenellated parapet, further decoration is supplied by a series of thirteenth century spandrels, the upper ones inverted. They probably came from the cathedral cloisters before they were re-modelled in the fifteenth century.

Inside on the ground floor is the chapel itself, heavily restored in the nineteenth century. The screen and ceiling are medieval although much renovated. In the 1930s the original stone altar slab was found face down in the floor when that was being renewed by the then master mason, 'Bert' Wheeler. It can now be seen, back in its proper position and in use whenever there is a service there. Upstairs, accessed by a stair turret in the north-west corner, was the vicars' library, the contents of which are now looked after in the cathedral library. At present, the chapel and library are at the disposal of the chaplain of Wells Cathedral School. The vicars choral use the chapel once a year to celebrate their commemoration day, even though the college itself was disbanded on 30th September 1936. This is followed by a celebratory breakfast banquet in Vicars' Hall. The twelve men, consisting of nine permanent members and three choral scholars all still live in the Close as do the three organists and others concerned with the day-to day-life of the cathedral.

Vicars' Hall is not open to the public except once a year on Heritage Open Day in September. It can however be booked for group lunches, dinners, and other events.

Adam Lock, Master Mason

Bishops of Wells

Athelm	909-923*	Aelfwine	997-999
Wulthelm 1	923-926*	Lyfing	999-1013*
Aelfeah	926-937	Aethelwine	1013-1023
Wulfhelm II	938-955	Brihtwig (or Merewit)	1024-1033*
Brithelm	956-974	Dudoc (or Duduc)	1033-1060
Cyneward	974-975	Giso	1061-1088
Sigar	975-997		

Bishops of Bath

John of Tours (or de Villula)	1088-1122*	Robert of Lewes	1136-1166*
Godfrey	1123-1135*	Reginald de Bohun (or Fitzjocelin)	1174-1191*

Bishops of Bath & Glastonbury

Savaric Fitzgeldewin	1192-1205*	Jocelin of Wells	1206-1219
		(then of Bath only)	1219-1242

Bishops of Bath & Wells

Roger of Salisbury	1244-1247*	Oliver King	1495-1503*
William Bytton I	1248-1264	Hadrian de Costello	1504-1518*
Walter Giffard	1265-1266*	Thomas Wolsey	1518-1523*
William Bytton II	1267-1274	John Clerke	1523-1541*
Robert Burnell	1275-1292	William Knight	1541-1547
William of March	1293-1302	William Barlow	1548-1553*
Walter Haselshaw	1302-1308	Gilbert Bourne	1554-1559*
John Drokensford (Droxford)	1309-1329	Gilbert Berkeley	1560-1581
Ralph of Shrewsbury	1329-1363	Thomas Godwyn	1584-1590*
John Barnet	1363-1366*	John Still	1593-1608
John Harewell	1367-1386	James Montague	1608-1616*
Walter Skitlaw	1386-1388*	Arthur Lake	1616-1626
Ralph Erghum	1388-1400	William Laud	1626-1628*
Richard Clifford	1400-1401*	Leonard Mawe	1628-1629*
Henry Bower	1401-1407*	Walter Curll	1629-1632*
Nicholas Bubwith	1407-1424	William Piers	1632-1670*
John Stafford	1425-1443*	Robert Creyghtone	1670-1672
Thomas Bekynton	1443-1465	Peter Mews	1673-1684*
Robert Stillington	1466-1491	Thomas Ken	1685-1691
Richard Fox	1492-1494*	Richard Kidder	1691-1703
		George Hooper	1704-1727

John Wynne	1727-1743*	Francis Underhill	1937-1943
Edward Wille	1743-1773*	John William	
Charles Moss	1774-1802*	Charles Wand	1943-1945*
Richard Beadon	1802-1824	Harold William	
George Henry Law	1824-1845	Bradfield	1946-1960
Richard Bagot	1845-1854*	Edward Barry	
Robert John (Eden),		Henderson	1960-1975
Baron Aukland	1854-1869	John Monier	
Lord Arthur Charles		Bickersteth	1975-1987
Hervey	1869-1894	George Carey	1987-1990
George Wyndham		James Thompson	1991-2001*
Kennion	1894-1921	Peter Bryan Price	2001-
St John Basil			
Wynne Willson	1921-1937	*not buried at Wells*	

Deans of Wells

Ivo	c.1140-c.1164	Walter Medeford	1413-1423
Richard of Spaxton	c.1164-1189	John Stafford	1423-1424
Alexander	1190-1213	John Forest	1425-1446
Leonius	1213-1216	Nicholas Carent	1446-1467
Ralph of Lechlade	1216-1219	William Whitham	1467-1472
Peter of Chichester	1219-1236	John Gunthorpe	1472-1498
William of Merton	1236-1241	William Cosyn	1498-1525
John Saracenus	1241-1253	Thomas Wynter	1525-1529
Giles of Bridport	1254-1256	Richard Woleman	1529-1537
Edward of Cnoll	1256-1284	Thomas Cromwell §	1537-1540
Thomas Bytton	1284-1292	William Fitzjames	
William Burnell	1292-1295	(or Fitzwilliam)	1540-1547
Walter Haselshaw	1295-1302	John Goodman	1548-1550
Henry Husee	1302-1305	William Turner	1551-1554
John de Godelee	1305-1333	John Goodman	
Richard of Bury	1333	(restored)	1554-1560
Wibert of Littleton	1334-1335	William Turner	
Walter of London	1335-1349	(restored)	1560-1568
Thomas Fastolf	1349-1350	Robert Weston §	1570-1573
John of Carleton	1350-1361	Valentine Dale §	1574-1589
Stephen Penpel	1361-1379	John Herbert §	1590-1602
John Fordham	1379-1381	Benjamin Heydon	1602-1607
Thomas Thebaud		Richard Meredeth	1607-1621
of Sudbury	1381-1396	Ralph Barlow	1621-1631
Henry Beaufort	1397-1398	George Warburton	1631-1641
Nicholas Slake	1398-1401	Walter Ralegh	1642-1644
Thomas Tuttebury	1401-1410	Robert Creyghtone	1660-1670
Richard Courtenay	1410-1413	Ralph Bathurst	1670-1704
Thomas Karneka	1413		

§ *a lay dean*

William Grahme
(after 1709: Graham) 1704-1713
Matthew Brailsford 1713-1733
Isaac Maddox 1733-1736
John Harris Bp. of
Llandaff 1736-1738
Samuel Creswicke 1739-1766
Lord Francis Seymour 1766-1799
George William Lukin 1799-1812
Hon. Henry Ryder also
Bp. of Gloucester,
1815-1824; Bp. of
Lichfield & Coventry,
1824-1836 1812-1831
Edmund Goodenough 1831-1845
Richard Jenkyns 1845-1854

George Henry
Sacheverell Johson 1854-1881
Edward Hayes Plumptre 1881-1891
Thomas William
Jex-Blake 1891-1911
Joseph Armitage
Robinson 1911-1933
Richard Henry Malden 1933-1950
Frederic Percival
Harton 1951-1958
Christopher Woodforde 1958-1962
Irven David Edwards 1962-1973
Patrick Reynolds
Mitchell 1973-1989
Richard Lewis 1990-2003
John Clarke 2004-

Dimensions

Total length	126.5m	415ft
Width across transepts (to outer wall face)	45.44m	149ft
Width of Transepts (east-west)	22.8m	74.8ft
Width of Nave and Aisles (from stone bench to stone bench)	20.12m	66ft (1 chain)
Length of Nave	45.57m	149.6ft
Width of West Front	45.72m	150ft
Height of Central Tower	55.47m	182ft
Height of Nave to Vaulting Rib	20.12m	66ft (1 chain)
Height of Quire	22.25m	73ft
Height of Western Towers	37.8m	124ft

Money Conversion

1/4d.	=	one quarter of one old penny
1d. (1 denarius)	=	one old penny
12d.	=	1s. (1 solidus) : one shilling (5p. in modern money)
20s.	=	£1 (libra) : one pound
One third of £1	=	1 noble (33p. in modern money)
Two thirds of £1	=	1 mark (67p. in modern money)

The mark was most used in the Middle Ages for large sums of money.

*The lists on pp.179-181 have been adapted and amended
from Colchester L. S., The New Bell's Guide to Wells Cathedral, (1987)*

The Friends of Wells Cathedral:
Major Grants to the Dean and Chapter

Pre 1938	£600	Four chapter house pinnacles	1980-82	£1,292	Masons' Yard equipment
1939-47	£1,200	Repairs to 4 more pinnacles		£1,000	Vicars' Hall kitchen
1949	£1,500	Chain Gate repairs		£10,000	Glass: N.Quire aisle & St Katherine's Ch.
1952	£1,000	Organ cleaning	1983-88	£42,000	Glazing Cloisters
	£700	Tracery E. Cloister		£149,504	Cloister restoration
1957-8	£1,350	Quire electrics		£17,400	Chapter House parapets
1959-61	£865	N. Trans. Pinnacles		£3,043	S. Quire Aisle glass
1962-3	£600	Vault C. house stairs		£5,000	Retroquire glass
1965	£1,000	Stairway window Chapter House		£10,000	Corpus Christi & St Stephen's glass
	£1,000	Re-casting bells		£22,500	'Risen Christ': David Wynne
1966-7	£3,000	Furniture nave sanctuary	1988-94	£635,638	Chapter House
1968	£1,950	Retroquire roof	1995	£18,551	Cloister garth
	£718	Nave chairs		£5,013	West Front angel
1969	£1,000	Masons' yard	1996	£63,604	Nave lighting
	£700	S. Trans. Roof parapet		£5,000	Organ
1970	£2,000	W. cloister	1996-8	£26,549	West Front angels
1971	£2,000	N. Trans. roof	1999	£6,360	West Front panel
	£500	Electrics	2000-1	£36,603	Chain Gate
1972	£2,000	S. Aisle parapet		£1,709	Redecorate Chapter House stairs
	£1,500	Vicars' Hall windows			
1973-5	£7,361	Organ case	2002	£1,788	Corpus Christi tiles
	£3,000	Organ restoration	2003	£2,322	Fire alarm
	£1,576	NW Tower scaffold.		£6,991	Hoist
	£2,500	Loudspeaker system	2004	£3,000	Crossing lights
	£1,700	S. Quire Aisle vault	2005-9	£25,381	Jesse window
1976	£5,605	Vicars' Hall & Chapel masonry		£1,838,639	Friends building
	£1,463	East End vaults	2010	£8,850	Clock winding system
	£1,000	Library			
1977	£6,750	East End vaults	2010-11	£5,582	New doors
1978	£6,700	S. Quire Aisle glass		£6,000	Organ loft CCTV
	£3,000	N. Quire Aisle vaults			
1979	£5,485	Vicars' Chapel roof			
1980-2	£28,000	West Cloister			
	£5,130	Fire precautions			
	£2,250	Vestments & soft furnishings			

The Friends have generously financed the publication of this book

Suggested Further Reading

Ayers, T., *The Medieval Stained Glass of Wells Cathedral* (2004)

Bailey, D. S., *Canonical Houses of Wells* (1982)

Binski, P., *Becket's Crown* (2004)

Colchester, L. S. (ed.), *Wells Cathedral, A History* (1982)

Colchester, L. S. and others, *A History of Wells Cathedral School* (1964)

Edwards, K., *The English Secular Cathedrals in the Middle Ages* (1967)

Foyle, A. and Pevsner, N., *The Buildings of England. Somerset: North and Bristol* (2011)

Historical Manuscripts Commission, *Calendar of the Manuscripts of the Dean and Chapter of Wells*, 2 vols. (1904, 1914)

Jewers, A. J., *Wells Cathedral: its monumental inscriptions and heraldry* (1892)

Meek, M., and Cowern, A., *The Wells Liberty and Bishop's Palace* (1982)

Pacey, A., *Medieval Architectural Drawing* (2007)

Rodwell, W., *Wells Cathedral Excavations and Structural Studies 1978-1993* (2001)

Rodwell, W., *The Archaeology of Churches* (2012)

Rodwell, W. and Neale, F., '"Begun While the Black Death Raged..." The Vicars' Close at Wells' in *Vicars Choral at English Cathedrals*, ed. Hall, R. and Stocker D., (2005), pp. 112-137.

Sampson, J., *Wells Cathedral West Front* (1998)

Tracy, C. (with a contribution from Budge, A.), *British Medieval Episcopal Thrones* (working title; forthcoming)

Watkin, A. (ed.), *Dean Cosyn and Wells Cathedral Miscellanea,* Somerset Record Society vol. 56 (1941)

Wilson, C., *The Gothic Cathedral* (1990)

Glossary

ABACUS   Flat stone topping a capital on a pillar (column or pier).

ABUTMENT   Meeting of an arch or vault with its solid lateral support, or the support itself.

AISLE   Internal space to the side of the main body of a building, separated from it by pillars, columns or piers.

AMBULATORY   Aisle round the sanctuary of a church for the purpose of processing or walking.

APSE   Curved or semi-circular end of a building, usually the far end of a church or chapel.

ARCADE   Series of arches supported by pillars or columns.

ASHLAR   Blocks of cut or worked stone with even faces and square edges.

BALLFLOWER   Decoration of three-petalled flower shaped round a ball.

BALUSTRADE   A rail comprised of *balusters:* pot-bellied vertical supports of a rail or coping.

BARREL VAULT   A simple vault also called 'tunnel vault' shaped as a continuous semi-circle, occasionally pointed.

BATTLEMENT   Originally a defensive parapet also used decoratively, composed of solid stone alternating with openings, also known as *crenellations*.

BAY   Interior space between two pillars or columns of an arch.

BLIND ARCADE   Series of arches on a wall, with no openings.

BOSS   Rounded projection at the intersection of ribs, usually carved.

BRACE   Subsidiary member of a structural frame to give added support, as in *wind-braces* or *scissor braces*.

BUTTERY   Store room off the screens passage of medieval house or college, used especially for drink.

BUTTRESS   Vertical member projecting from a wall to stabilize it or to resist the lateral thrust of an arch, roof or vault.

CADAVER   A naked figure effigy on a monument, also called a *gisant*.

CAPITAL   The head, usually carved feature of a pillar or column.

CHEVRON   V shaped or zigzag moulding common in Romanesque style.

CINQUEFOIL   A five-lobed or curved opening of an arch.

CLERESTORY   Top storey of a church, usually the third level, with windows.

CONDUIT   A water pipe or public water source.

CORBEL   Projecting stone often carved supporting a structure above.

CRENELLATIONS   Defensive openings on a parapet (cf battlements).

CUSPS   Points where two curves meet.

Glossary

DIOCESE The area or see administered by a (diocesan) bishop.

FAN-VAULTING Vault of a series of cones, half or quarter cones, decorated with blind tracery: Perpendicular (third phase) of Gothic architecture.

FINIAL Top ornament of spire, gable, pinnacle or roof-ridge.

FLEURON Medieval flower or leaf carving, often rectilinear.

GRISAILLE Painting in monochrome, usually in shades of grey, on glass

HEADSTOP Carved head end of a hood-mould or label.

HOOD-MOULD Projected moulding over an arch.

KEEL MOULDING Round moulding brought to a point like a ship's keel.

LABEL Projected square or horizontal moulding over an arch or window.

LIGHT Section of a window defined by uprights.

MULLION Vertical stone between window lights.

OGEE An 'S' shaped curve used most in the 14th century.

PISCINA A basin for washing Communion vessels or hands.

PYX A receptical where the Host (Communion bread and wine) is kept.

QUARRY A small square or diamond shaped pane of glass with supporting lead strips.

REREDOS A screen behind and above an altar, often painted and carved.

RUBBLE Unworked or rough stone.

SPANDREL A 'triangular' shape between two adjoining arches or between the head of an arch and its extended vertical sides.

STRING COURSE Horizontal moulding projecting from a wall, usually with a rolled edge.

TIERCERON Additional decorative ribs springing from the corners of a bay.

TRACERY Openwork pattern of masonry particularly in the upper part of an opening.

TRIFORIUM The middle storey of a large church used as an arcaded passageway.

TYMPANUM The head of a blind arch or doorway often filled with carving.

UNDERCROFT The vaulted room beneath the main room of a medieval building.

VOUSSOIRS Wedge-shaped stones forming an arch: sometimes carved.

Index